Grand Cayman Travel Guide 2024-2025

Your Ultimate Guide to Caribbean Bliss, Adventure, And Coastal Splendor

A M JACOB

Copyright © 2023 by A M JACOB

All rights reserved. No part of this publication may be reproduced, distributed, or transmitted in any form or by any means, including photocopying, recording, or other electronic or mechanical methods, without the prior written permission of the publisher, except in the case of brief quotations embodied in critical reviews and certain other noncommercial uses

Table Of Content

Introduction   7
Chapter One: Planning for Your Grand Cayman Adventure   11
    Amazing Fun Facts About Grand Cayman   11
    History and Significance   13
    Best Time to Visit Grand Cayman   16
    Visa Requirements   19
    Packing Essentials   22
    Local laws and customs   27
Chapter 2: Getting There and Around   31
    Getting To Grand Cayman   31
    Getting Around The Island   34
Chapter Three: Communication in Grand Cayman   39
Chapter Four: Budget-Friendly Accomodations   49
    Westin Grand Cayman   49
    Grand Cayman Marriott   51
    Sunshine Suites Resort   52
    The Ritz-Carlton   54
    The Locale Hotel   57
    Wyndham Reef Resort   58
    The island Club   61
    The Caribbean Club   64
    The Grand Cayman Resort   66
    Villas of The Galleon   69
Chapter Five: Must Visit Attractions   **71**
    Hell   71

Porto di Georgetown (Port of George Town) 73
Cayman Crystal Caves 75
Seven Mile Beach 77
Stingray City 79
Queen Elizabeth II Botanic Park 81
Starfish Point 84
Cemetery Beach and Reef 86
Cayman Turtle Centre 88
Kittiwake Shipwreck & Artificial Reef 90

Chapter Six: Grand Cayman Cultural Insights 93

Embracing Grand Cayman Culture and traditions 93

Events and festivals 97

Swashbuckling Extravaganza 97
Carnival at Batabano 98
A Gastronomic Extravaganza on Cayman 99
Cayman Islands Carnival 101
CayFilm 102
Cayman Arts Festival 103
Cayman's National Heroes Day 104
Tips for Attending Grand Cayman Events and Festivals 105

Chapter Seven: Grand Cayman Culinary Delight 109

Grand Cayman Cafes and Restaurants 109
Must Try Grand Cayman island Dishes 113
Shopping Centers and Street Markets 124
Tips for Dining and Shopping In Grand Cayman 129

Chapter Eight: Practical Advice For Visitors 133

Currency and Banking information	133
Safety precautions	137
Contact and Emergency Information	142
Souvenirs to Bring Home	146
Conclusion	**151**
Travel Journal	**156**

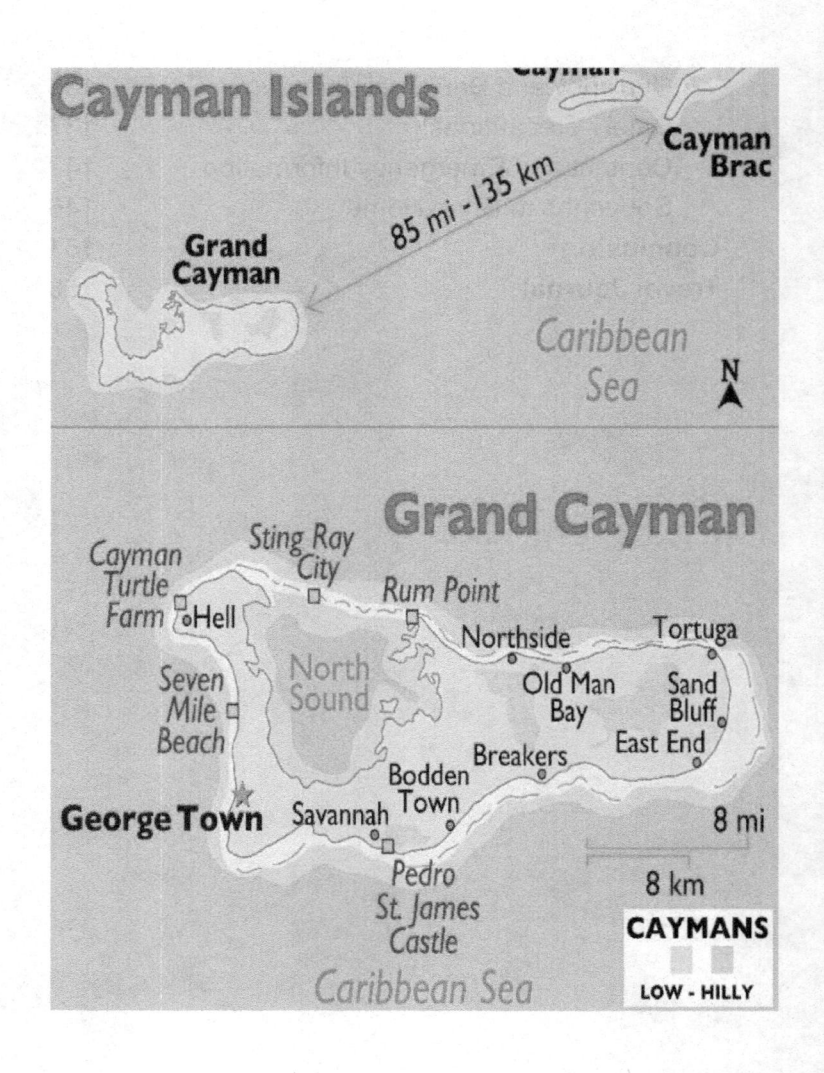

Cayman Islands

Cayman Brac

85 mi - 135 km

Grand Cayman

Caribbean Sea

N

Grand Cayman

- Cayman Turtle Farm
- Hell
- Sting Ray City
- Rum Point
- Northside
- Tortuga
- North Sound
- Old Man Bay
- Sand Bluff
- Seven Mile Beach
- Breakers
- East End
- Bodden Town
- **George Town**
- Savannah
- Pedro St. James Castle

Caribbean Sea

8 mi
8 km

CAYMANS
LOW - HILLY

Introduction

Welcome to Grand Cayman, a tropical paradise with crystal-clear seas, powdery sand beaches, and an atmosphere that perfectly combines leisure and action. Our Grand Cayman Travel Guide strives to be your compass as you begin on your adventure to this wonderful island, guiding you through a tapestry of experiences that will leave you with cherished memories.

Discovering Grand Cayman: A Natural and Cultural Symphony

Grand Cayman, the largest of the three Cayman Islands, spreads like a brilliant canvas painted with hues of azure, emerald, and golden sunshine in the western Caribbean Sea. Let's dig into the cultural tapestry that makes Grand Cayman a distinct and welcome place before you step foot on this sun-kissed refuge.

Cultural Kaleidoscope: A Traditions Melting Pot

The cultural environment of Grand Cayman is a balanced combination of influences that reflects the variety of its people. The island's customs, music, and food are heavily inspired by Jamaican, British, and other Caribbean cultures. The Caymanian people's kindness is tangible, enticing you to immerse yourself in their way of life.

A Look Back in Time: From Pirates to Paradise

Take a trip back in time as Grand Cayman exposes its fascinating past. The island, once a shelter for pirates and a stopover for adventurers, has transformed into a modern-day paradise. Discover the stories of shipwrecks, maritime legends, and the indomitable character that has turned Grand Cayman into the Caribbean's gem.

Faith and Spirituality: Respect for Different Beliefs

Various faiths dwell together in this tropical sanctuary. The island is dominated by Christianity, with churches dotting the landscape, but it also celebrates diversity, inviting inhabitants and tourists of all faith origins. The spiritual ambiance is woven into the fabric of daily life, adding to the sense of calm that pervades Grand Cayman.

How to Navigate the Practicalities of Currency and Legal Harmony

As you plan your trip, become acquainted with the Cayman Islands Dollar (KYD), the national currency. Banking and financial services are reliable, ensuring that your transactions run smoothly. You'll find a dedication to safety and order in this picturesque haven, with legislation meant to protect the island's natural beauty and maintain a sense of tranquility.

Your Grand Cayman Adventure Is About to Begin

We welcome you to turn the pages of our book as you begin on your journey, armed with insights on Grand Cayman's colorful culture, historic history, and practical considerations. Each chapter leads you to magnificent beaches, exhilarating experiences, and the heart of Caymanian friendliness. So pack your sense of wonder and let Grand Cayman's charm unroll before you—a location where every moment is a brushstroke on the canvas of a beautiful holiday. Hello and welcome to paradise!

Grand Cayman Island Is a Lovely Place To Be. You will Definitely Enjoy Your Stay If You Follow The Guidelines In This Book.

Chapter One: Planning for Your Grand Cayman Adventure

Amazing Fun Facts About Grand Cayman

1. **Stingray City**: Stingray City, a one-of-a-kind attraction on Grand Cayman, allows guests to interact with friendly southern stingrays in shallow water. It's one of the few spots in the world where you may get up close to these intriguing creatures.

2. **Seven Mile Beach**: Despite its moniker, Seven Mile Beach in Grand Cayman is approximately 5.5 miles long. However, it is routinely recognized as one of the top beaches in the Caribbean due to its beautiful white sand and crystal-clear water.

3. **Underwater Sculpture Park**: Grand Cayman has the world's first underwater sculpture park, which is located off the coast of George Town. The park, designed by artist Jason deCaires Taylor, has over 500 life-size sculptures buried beneath the water that serve as artificial reefs and aquatic ecosystems.

4. **Hell**: On Grand Cayman, there is a site named "Hell" notable for its peculiar limestone formations resembling jagged black rocks. Visitors can mail postcards bearing the iconic "Hell" postmark from the local post office.

5. **Bioluminescent Bay**: In Grand Cayman's North Sound, microorganisms known as dinoflagellates generate a blue-green light when disturbed, producing a spectacular glow-in-the-dark effect in the water at night.

6. **Green Sea Turtles**: Grand Cayman is an important nesting location for green sea turtles. At the Cayman Turtle Centre, visitors may learn about conservation efforts and even help release turtles.

7. **Cayman Crystal caverns**: These breathtaking limestone caverns on Grand Cayman contain fascinating formations, subterranean lakes, and crystal-clear pools. Guided tours allow guests to explore this fascinating underground environment.

8. **Pedro St. James Castle**: Pedro St. James Castle, known as the "birthplace of democracy in the Cayman Islands," is a historic monument on Grand Cayman. It is one of the oldest buildings in the Caribbean, providing insight into the island's rich past.

9. **Mastic track**: Grand Cayman is home to the Mastic Trail, a picturesque hiking track that runs through old-growth forest and mangrove swamplands. It's a fantastic opportunity to explore the island's natural beauty and variety.

10. **cuisine Delights**: Grand Cayman has a rich cuisine scene inspired by Caribbean, British, and international tastes. Visitors may enjoy wonderful seafood, fresh tropical fruits, and traditional cuisine like conch fritters and jerk chicken.

These amusing facts highlight the distinct and various attractions that make Grand Cayman such an intriguing place to visit.

History and Significance

Grand Cayman, with its sun-kissed beaches and turquoise oceans, is more than simply a tropical paradise; it is a living witness to a rich and diverse past that has sculpted this Caribbean treasure into the paradise it is today. Take a trip through time as you walk the beaches of this gorgeous island, where legends of pirates, maritime exploits, and cultural development mingle to form a riveting story of Grand Cayman's past.

Nature's Bounty and Early Settlers: Indigenous Foundations

Long before European explorers set foot on the Caribbean, indigenous peoples such as the Lucayans and Tainos called the islands home. With its plentiful marine life and verdant sceneries, Grand Cayman supplied nourishment and a healthy home. The original residents left behind artifacts and implements, which are today preserved as windows into Grand Cayman's ancient history.

Pirates, Wreckers, and Piracy's Golden Age

The 17th and 18th centuries heralded a new period of seafaring, with Grand Cayman becoming an infamous sanctuary for pirates and wreckers. The island's hidden coves and hazardous reefs were perfect hiding places for buccaneers fleeing imperial warships. According to legend, great pirates such as Blackbeard and Edward Teach formerly sailed these waterways, creating a legacy of mystery and intrigue.

Economic Transformations from the Sea to the Sugar Plantations

As the Golden Age of Piracy came to an end, Grand Cayman began a new chapter in its history. The island's economy transitioned from illegal to more respectable enterprises, with marine turtles playing an important part. Turtle fishing and processing were profitable enterprises, supplying economic sustenance to the growing population. The Cayman Turtle Centre, a living homage to this bygone period, still displays relics of turtle fishing traditions.

British Colonial Influence: Cayman Islands Acquire Crown Colony

Grand Cayman was taken over by the British in the 18th century, ushering in a long period of colonial rule. In 1863, the island became a Crown Colony, encouraging stability and government. The British influence is seen in Grand Cayman's architecture, governance structures, and legal systems, which continue to affect the island today.

Modern Development: From Isolation to Global Appeal

Grand Cayman went from relative obscurity to a sought-after resort in the twentieth century. In the 1950s, the building of Owen Roberts International Airport cleared the door for enhanced accessibility, converting the island into a tourism and international banking powerhouse. Grand Cayman is now not only a tropical paradise, but also a bustling commercial and hospitality hub.

Facing Natural Disasters: Resilience and Recovery

The history of Grand Cayman is also defined by its perseverance in the face of catastrophic calamities. Hurricanes have repeatedly devastated the island, putting its residents to the test. Despite this, the people of Grand Cayman have shown a remarkable capacity to repair and rejuvenate, displaying an indomitable spirit that has echoed down the years.

Know that every grain of sand beneath your feet bears tales of a compelling past as you explore Grand Cayman's sunny beaches and colorful towns. The island's history weaves together to make a gripping tale that sets the scene for your own Grand Cayman journey, a combination of indigenous legacies, pirate mythology, colonial impact, and current development.

Best Time to Visit Grand Cayman

Grand Cayman's sun-kissed beaches and turquoise waters entice travelers all year, but picking the right time to visit may boost your experience from wonderful to utterly stunning. The climate of the island, seasonal variations, and the ebb and flow of visitors all generate various windows of opportunity.

Let us unlock the secrets of timing and reveal the finest times to visit Grand Cayman's brilliant coastlines.

Brilliance in High Season: December to April

If you're looking for the pinnacle of Caribbean perfection, Grand Cayman shines brightly from December to April. This time of year shows the island at its most beautiful, with mild temperatures, little rain, and soft trade breezes caressing the palm-fringed coastlines. The beautiful sky and calm waters create an excellent setting for sunbathers and water sports enthusiasts.

Grand Cayman comes alive during the busy season. The calendar is jam-packed with exciting events and festivals, and the island's attractions and activities are in full swing. Dive into the crystal-clear seas to discover coral reefs filled with marine life, or simply relax on Seven Mile Beach under the warm Caribbean sun. Expect a lively atmosphere and a plethora of food and entertainment options, since this is the island's busiest time.

The Low Season Charms of Serene Escape: May to November

For those looking for a more serene retreat, the low season, which runs from May to November, has a distinct attraction. While there is more rain and a larger likelihood of seeing short tropical showers during this time, the lush scenery and fewer visitors offer an intimate backdrop for those preferring a more isolated experience.

The low season reveals Grand Cayman's natural beauty at its peak. The island is covered with lush flora, and rain showers provide a welcome freshness to the air. This is an excellent time for nature enthusiasts since the plants and wildlife are in full bloom, providing a magnificent backdrop for exploring. The low season also provides a chance for budget-conscious tourists, since hotels and activities may be less expensive at this time.

How to Navigate the Shoulder Seasons of November and May

The transitional months of November and May provide a golden spot between the peak and low seasons. You may enjoy a wonderful combination of great weather and less crowds during these shoulder seasons. While there may be some rain, the island is either awakening or winding down, giving a gentler vibe for those looking for a blend of lively energy and serene escape.

The optimum time to visit Grand Cayman is determined by your interests and priorities. Whether you visit during the peak season for its picture-perfect weather and bustling environment, the low season for a more tranquil retreat, or the shoulder seasons for a more balanced experience, Grand Cayman will greet you with a dazzling welcome. Consider the seasonal differences and connect your visit with the rhythm of this Caribbean paradise as you arrange your island excursion to make your stay really unique.

Visa Requirements

The anticipation of traveling to the sun-drenched shores of Grand Cayman is enticing, and understanding the visa requirements is a critical step in ensuring a smooth entry into this Caribbean paradise. Grand Cayman, as a British Overseas Territory, welcomes tourists from all over the world, and understanding the visa procedures will ensure a stress-free and enjoyable vacation.

Visa-Free Entry: A Warm Welcome

The good news for many visitors is that Grand Cayman welcomes them without requiring a visa. Visa-free entrance for short visits is available to citizens of various countries, including the United States, the

United Kingdom, Canada, and the majority of European nations. Typically, this permits for a 30-day vacation, but it's critical to double-check the precise entrance criteria based on your nationality.

Options for Extending Your Caymanian Adventure

If your heart desires a longer stay beyond the first 30 days, Grand Cayman provides visa extensions. These requests are handled by the Cayman Islands Immigration Department, and applications must be submitted before your first entrance time expires. Exploring extension options can improve your Grand Cayman experience, whether you're drawn to the rich culture, aquatic marvels, or simply want to absorb the island's calm for a little longer.

Visa-Required Countries: A Few Points to Consider

While citizens of many countries are granted visa-free entry, it is important to examine the exact criteria for your nationality. Some travelers, particularly those from countries not on the list above, may be required to get a visa before arriving in Grand Cayman. This entails submitting an application well in advance of your anticipated trip dates to the nearest British

Embassy or Consulate. It is best to start this procedure as soon as possible to avoid any potential delays.

Prerequisites for Easy Entry: Other Than Visas

Other entrance procedures must be considered in addition to visa concerns for a smooth arrival in Grand Cayman. These are some examples:

1. **Passport Validity:** Make sure your passport is valid for at least six months beyond the day you want to leave Grand Cayman.

2. **Return Ticket:** Immigration officials may want documentation of a return or onward ticket, confirming your intend to depart the island within the duration allowed.

3. **Adequate Funds:** Be prepared to show proof of adequate financial resources to fund your stay, guaranteeing you can enjoy your time on the island pleasantly.

Entry Points to Owen Roberts International Airport

Owen Roberts International Airport is the principal entrance point for most visitors to Grand Cayman. When you arrive, immigration agents will process your admission, examine your documents, and issue the relevant permits based on your travel plans.

As you plan your trip to Grand Cayman, take in mind the visa requirements and entrance procedures to ensure a smooth and pleasurable journey. Whether you want to experience the excitement of undersea exploration, the serenity of beautiful beaches, or the colorful local culture, Grand Cayman welcomes you with open arms and is eager to make your stay unforgettable.

Packing Essentials

Packing becomes an art form as you prepare to leave on your Grand Cayman adventure, merging comfort, style, and practicality to ensure you're well-prepared for the tropical delights that await. From sun-kissed beach days to undersea expeditions, strategic packing will enrich your trip to this Caribbean gem. Here's a list of must-have goods to guarantee you're prepared for every aspect of your Grand Cayman vacation.

1. Sunscreen and Skin Protection: Protecting Your Skin

The sun is a bright friend on Grand Cayman, and while bathing in its warmth is a pleasure, protection is essential. Pack a high SPF sunscreen to protect your skin from the rays of the Caribbean sun. Bring a wide-brimmed hat, sunglasses, and lightweight clothes with long sleeves for extra protection during peak hours.

2. Dive into the Blue with Swimwear and Snorkeling Gear

The crystalline seas of the island beckon, and swimwear is a must. Comfortable and attractive swimwear is essential whether you're relaxing on Seven Mile Beach or exploring the vivid coral reefs. Pack your snorkeling gear if you have it, so you may explore the underwater delights at your own time.

3. Wearing Lightweight Clothes: Embracing Island Casual

The relaxed environment of Grand Cayman necessitates airy, lightweight attire. To remain cool in the tropical heat, bring comfortable shorts, dresses, and breathable materials. Remember to bring a light jacket or sweater for chilly evenings or air-conditioned areas.

4. From Sand to Street **Comfortable Footwear

Versatile footwear is vital for exploring sandy beaches and attractive neighborhoods. Bring comfortable footwear for beach excursions and flip-flops for leisurely walks. Consider wearing durable water shoes for rough terrain if you intend to explore the island's natural treasures.

5. Capturing Subaquatic Memories with an Underwater Camera

Grand Cayman's underwater scenery are a photographer's dream. Make sure you have a waterproof or underwater camera to record the rich marine life, gorgeous coral formations, and your amazing underwater encounters.

6. Using Travel Adapters in Paradise

Pack the necessary travel adapters to keep your electrical gadgets charged. The electrical outlets in Grand Cayman are the same as those in the United States and Canada (Type A and B), but it's always a good idea to double-check and bring the required adapters for your equipment.

7. Insect Repellent: Keeping Uninvited Guests at Bay

While the Caribbean is not known for its pest problems, it is a good idea to bring insect repellant with you for increased comfort during outdoor activities, especially in the nights. It is sufficient to use a tiny, travel-sized bottle.

8. Reef-Friendly Toiletries: Environmental Protection

Grand Cayman prioritizes environmental protection, notably the preservation of its coral reefs. Bring reef-safe sunscreen and toiletries to help the island meet its commitment to sustainability.

9. Staying Hydrated Responsibly with a Reusable Water Bottle

Working in the Caribbean heat may be deceptively thirsty. Carry a reusable water bottle with you to remain hydrated, and consider a collapsible style for ease of use while exploring.

10. **First Aid Kit: Dealing with the Unexpected

A little first-aid kit can be a traveler's best friend. Include necessary items such as sticky bandages, pain remedies, motion sickness medicine, and any personal prescriptions.

11. Daypack that is lightweight and convenient for excursions

For day trips and excursions, a compact, lightweight daypack is useful. It can easily carry necessities such as water, sunscreen, a camera, and any mementos picked up along the route.

12. **Travel Insurance Provides Peace of Mind

Secure comprehensive travel insurance before stepping foot on the island. This protects you against unforeseen situations like medical problems and trip cancellations, giving you peace of mind throughout your Grand Cayman journey.

When making your packing list for Grand Cayman, imagine a Caribbean capsule wardrobe that combines elegance, comfort, and usefulness. Everything you bring, from sun protection to underwater exploration, adds to the canvas of your island trip. As you zip up your luggage, imagine the sun on your face, the beach between your toes, and the immersing pleasures that await you in Grand Cayman's bright embrace.

Local laws and customs

While on your Grand Cayman vacation, you will not only discover the beautiful scenery of the Caribbean, but you will also be introduced to a society with a rich tapestry of local laws and customs. Understanding and appreciating these cultural distinctions will not only assure a pleasant and pleasurable vacation, but will also develop a stronger relationship with Grand Cayman's kind people.

Legal Landscape: Respectfully Navigating Local Laws

As a British Overseas Territory, Grand Cayman has a legal system that combines British law with its own distinctive legislation. Visitors should be aware of the following crucial components of local laws:

1. **Driving Regulations:** Driving in Grand Cayman is on the left side of the road. Visitors may use their legal home country driver's license for up to six months, but speed restrictions and traffic laws must be followed.

2. **Drug Laws:** It is unlawful to possess or consume illicit narcotics, including marijuana.

Violations of drug laws can result in harsh consequences, therefore it's critical to avoid engaging in any illicit activity.

3. **Respect for Marine Life:** Because Grand Cayman values its marine life, injuring or collecting coral, sea animals, or artifacts is strictly forbidden. This environmental protection pledge is part of the island's commitment to conserving its natural beauty.

4. **Conservation Efforts:** Grand Cayman prioritizes environmental conservation. As a tourist, you can help by respecting designated protected areas and doing eco-friendly behaviors like applying reef-safe sunscreen.

5. **Public Nudity:** While swimwear is permitted on beaches, public nudity is not. It is critical to observe cultural standards and dress correctly in public places.

Cultural Etiquette: Gracefully Accepting Caymanian Customs

The culture of Grand Cayman is one of warmth and friendliness, and tourists may enhance their experience by adopting local habits. Here are some standards for cultural etiquette:

1. **Greetings and Politeness:** In Grand Cayman, a simple "hello" and a smile go a long way. Politeness is

highly prized, therefore using "sir" or "ma'am" to address individuals is considered polite.

2. **Respect for Elders:** Elder respect is an important aspect of Caymanian society. When engaging with older people, maintain a pleasant approach and pay attention.

3. **Sunday observation:** Traditionally, Sundays are a day of relaxation and religious observation. Many companies close or operate on limited hours, and loud activities are often prohibited in order to honor the Sabbath.

4. **Island Time:** Grand Cayman works on a more leisurely schedule known as "island time." Embrace the slower pace and allow yourself to unwind away from the daily grind.

5. **Friendliness:** The people of Grand Cayman are noted for their warmth and friendliness. Conversations with locals and a genuine interest in their culture might result in great friendships and unforgettable experiences.

Casual Elegance with Respect is the dress code.

Grand Cayman's dress code is usually informal and laidback, reflecting the island's laid-back lifestyle. Some venues and restaurants, especially in the nights, may have a more formal dress code. It's a good idea to double-check precise criteria for any scheduled trips to ensure you're dressed suitably.

Cultural Events and Festivals: Immersion in Local Festivities

Participating in local events and festivals is a fantastic opportunity to immerse yourself in Grand Cayman's colorful culture. Events such as the Batabano Carnival, Pirates Week Festival, and local music performances offer insights into the island's past and current character.

You will not only conform to Grand Cayman's requirements but also establish significant ties with the community if you navigate the local laws and traditions with respect and transparency. Embracing the island's cultural tapestry enriches your experience, resulting in cherished memories that stretch beyond the breathtaking vistas and into the heart of Caymanian friendliness.

Chapter 2: Getting There and Around

Getting To Grand Cayman

Getting to Grand Cayman is a seamless and enjoyable experience, with several convenient transportation options available to travelers. Whether arriving by air or sea, visitors can access the island with ease, ready to embark on an unforgettable Caribbean adventure.

By Air:

Arriving by air is the most common and convenient way to reach Grand Cayman, with Owen Roberts International Airport (GCM) serving as the island's primary gateway. Situated in George Town, the airport offers direct flights from various international destinations, including the United States, Canada, the United Kingdom, and other Caribbean islands.

International Flights:

Travelers from North America can choose from numerous direct flights to Grand Cayman from major cities such as Miami, New York, Atlanta, Toronto, and Chicago. Airlines offering direct services include American Airlines, Delta Air Lines, United Airlines, and WestJet, among others.

European Flights:
European travelers can access Grand Cayman via direct flights from London, with British Airways operating regular services to the island. Alternatively, travelers can connect through major European hubs such as Frankfurt or Amsterdam to reach Grand Cayman with one stopover.

Caribbean Flights:
For travelers originating from other Caribbean islands, regional airlines such as Cayman Airways, Caribbean Airlines, and interCaribbean Airways offer convenient connections to Grand Cayman from destinations like Jamaica, the Bahamas, and the Dominican Republic.

Upon arrival at Owen Roberts International Airport, travelers will go through customs and immigration procedures before collecting their luggage and exiting the terminal. Taxis, private shuttles, and rental cars are readily available at the airport to transport visitors to their accommodations or desired destinations across the island.

By Sea:
While less common than air travel, arriving in Grand Cayman by sea offers a unique and scenic experience for travelers. Cruise ships regularly visit the island,

docking at the bustling George Town Harbor located on the western coast of Grand Cayman.

Cruise Ships:

Numerous cruise lines, including Royal Caribbean, Carnival Cruise Line, and Norwegian Cruise Line, include Grand Cayman on their itineraries. Visitors disembark at the port and are greeted by a vibrant waterfront area filled with shops, restaurants, and excursion opportunities.

Ferry Services:

Travelers from nearby islands such as Jamaica or Cuba can also reach Grand Cayman via ferry services. While less frequent than air travel, ferry services provide an alternative option for those seeking a slower-paced journey to the island.

Regardless of the mode of transportation chosen, travelers to Grand Cayman are greeted with warm hospitality and stunning natural beauty upon arrival. With its convenient accessibility and welcoming atmosphere, Grand Cayman invites visitors to embark on an unforgettable Caribbean getaway filled with adventure, relaxation, and discovery.

Getting Around The Island

The temptation of discovery beckons as you tread onto the sun-drenched coastline of Grand Cayman. Navigating the island's transportation choices is an important part of planning your ideal Caribbean vacation. Understanding the types of transportation in Grand Cayman helps your tour across this tropical paradise, from sandy beaches to cultural sites.

1. **Car Rentals: Independence on Four Wheels

Car rentals are a popular and practical option for individuals who want the flexibility to explore at their own speed. Numerous rental businesses, both foreign and domestic, provide a variety of automobiles to fit a variety of needs. Driving on the left side of the road is the norm in Grand Cayman, and the island's well-maintained road network makes it simple to get about. Car rentals allow you to get off the usual route, uncover hidden gems, and enjoy the magnificent sceneries of the island.

2. **Taxis: Convenient Transportation

Taxis are a convenient and pleasant mode of transportation in Grand Cayman. Whether you need a trip from the airport to your hotel or a quick transit to a specific location, cabs are a simple alternative. It's best to agree on a fee with the driver before leaving, and taxi services are widely utilized on the island for both short and long trips.

3. **The Island's Pulse: Public Buses

The "George Town Shuttle," Grand Cayman's public bus system, provides an economical and intimate viewpoint on island life. While not as broad or regular as in larger cities, buses run on particular routes, stopping at strategic points. This low-cost alternative is great for individuals who like a slower pace and the opportunity to interact with the local community.

4. **Bicycles and Scooters: Recreational Exploration

Grand Cayman is ideal for exploring on two wheels, thanks to its level topography and appealing coastline roads. Many rental companies provide bicycles and scooters, allowing tourists to experience the island's natural beauty at a more leisurely pace. This environmentally friendly alternative is especially enjoyable for seaside trips and visiting local communities.

5. **Seaside Serenity: Water Taxis

The coastal appeal of Grand Cayman extends to its water taxis, which provide a picturesque and leisurely way of transportation around the beach. Water taxis are available for hiring, providing a unique perspective of the island's breathtaking scenery. A water taxi journey is a quiet and unique experience, whether you're commuting between waterfront locales or simply want to absorb the beauty of the Caribbean Sea.

6. **Stress-Free Adventures with Guided Tours & Excursions

Guided tours and excursions provide a customized experience of Grand Cayman's attractions for people who want stress-free discovery. From snorkeling expeditions to cultural tours, a variety of operators provide guided activities to suit a variety of interests and tastes. These trips frequently include transportation, enabling you to focus on enjoying the event while leaving the practicalities in the hands of professionals.

7. **Exploring Sister Islands: Island Hopping

While this article focuses on Grand Cayman, it's worth mentioning that the Cayman Islands are made up of three islands. Domestic flights and ferry services link the islands, giving opportunity for unique excursions and discoveries for those interested in venturing beyond Grand Cayman.

8. **Walking: Paradise Strolls

Walking is a pleasant means of transportation in some regions, particularly near major tourist spots and beaches. The island's small size and pedestrian-friendly regions make it simple to explore on foot, whether you're wandering through the colorful alleys of George Town or strolling along Seven Mile Beach.

Consider the nature of your plan and the experiences you want to embrace as you negotiate transportation in Grand Cayman. Whether you're cruising along coastal roads in a rented car, savoring the sea breeze on a water taxi, or immersing yourself in local culture via public buses, the island's transportation options are designed to enhance your journey through Grand Cayman's enchanting landscapes and vibrant culture.

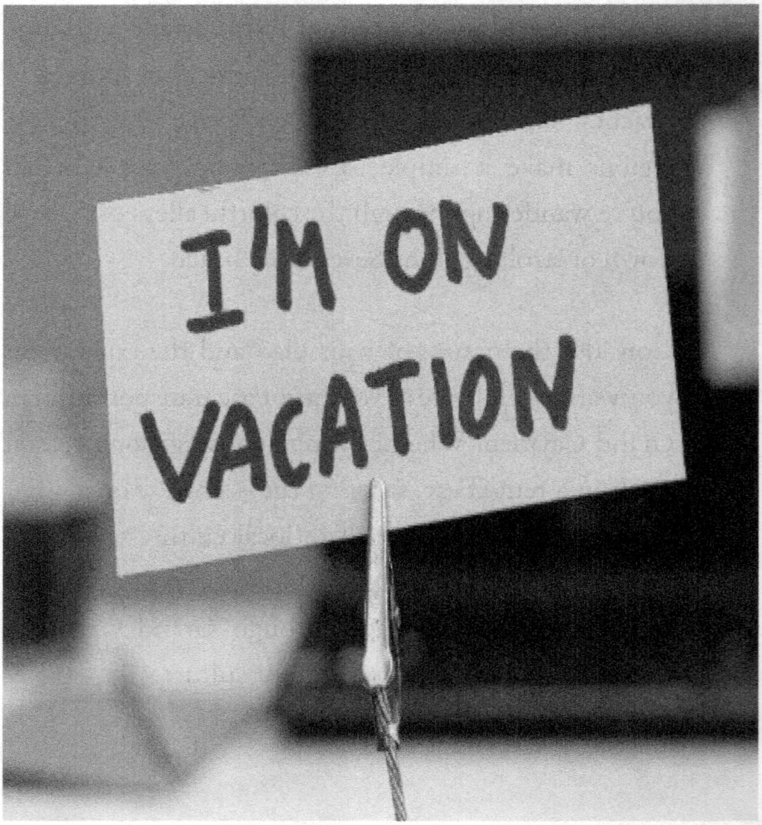
I'M ON
VACATION

Chapter Three: Communication in Grand Cayman

As you go off on your Grand Cayman journey, clear communication will improve every element of your stay on this Caribbean treasure. Understanding the communication environment facilitates a seamless and comfortable voyage across the sun-soaked landscapes and lively culture of Grand Cayman, from staying in touch with loved ones to navigating local peculiarities.

1. **A Caribbean Melody is the language.

The official language of the Cayman Islands, including Grand Cayman, is English. The language familiarity provides visitors with a secure basis, making conversation simple and uncomplicated. English proficiency is prevalent, whether requesting directions, engaging in local conversations, or participating in tours, creating a welcome environment for international visitors.

2. **Caymanian Expressions: Embracing Local Phrases

While English is widely spoken, learning a few local words can give you a sense of cultural immersion.

Visitors who show an interest in their culture are appreciated by Grand Caymanians, and a cordial "Caymanian hello" or "yah mon" (a Caribbean word for agreement or recognition) can inspire warm smiles and friendship.

3. **Financial Conversations on Currency and Payments

The Cayman Islands Dollar (KYD) is the island's official currency. It's a good idea to become acquainted with the local currency and exchange rates, especially if you want to make purchases or conduct transactions outside of main tourist regions. Although credit cards are generally accepted, it's a good idea to keep some local money on hand for smaller places or sellers.

4. **Staying Connected with Mobile Networks and SIM Cards

The mobile network infrastructure in Grand Cayman is dependable and well-developed. Visitors can utilize international roaming services with the mobile operator of their native country. Alternatively, getting a local SIM card is a simple way to stay connected for individuals looking for a more cost-effective choice. Prepaid SIM cards with data, call, and text capabilities are available from local mobile service providers, letting you to travel the island with ease.

5. **Internet Access: Virtual Exploration

The island's friendliness extends to the digital sphere, with free Wi-Fi available in many lodgings, restaurants, and public locations. Staying connected to the internet is a smooth experience in Grand Cayman, whether you're sharing your sun-soaked beach moments with pals or researching local activities.

6. **Postal Services: Greetings from the Tropics

The island's postal services are dependable for individuals who want to share the beauty of Grand Cayman with loved ones. Post offices are placed in strategic locations around the city, notably George Town, and provide international shipping services. Sending a bit of paradise to friends or family is a great way to extend the enchantment of your Grand Cayman vacation.

7. **Emergency Services: Safety Navigation

While the need for emergency assistance is uncommon, knowing the local emergency contact information is critical. 911 is the Cayman Islands' emergency number for police, fire, and medical help. The well-established healthcare facilities of Grand Cayman, particularly the Cayman Islands Hospital, offer extensive medical services to visitors.

8. **Weather Updates: Managing Tropical Weather

Given Grand Cayman's tropical environment, being updated about weather conditions is recommended, especially if you want to indulge in outdoor activities. Local news networks, radio stations, and internet weather services give frequent weather reports, allowing you to arrange your travels around the island's environment.

9. **Tourist Information Centers: Professional Advice

Tourist Information Centers are strategically positioned across Grand Cayman, providing tourists with important advice and direction. Staff that are knowledgeable with the area's attractions, cultural events, and transportation choices can help. These centers are great places to get maps, brochures, and insider information to help you make the most of your visit.

10. **Cultural Awareness: Respectful Communication

Despite the fact that English is the official language, learning and appreciating the local culture help to make meaningful connections. Polite welcomes, expressions of thanks, and genuine interest in the local way of life go a long way toward developing constructive connection. Embracing the local culture improves your entire experience and leaves you with lasting recollections of your time in Grand Cayman.

In Grand Cayman, communication is a seamless combination of linguistic familiarity, cultural respect, and modern connectedness. Effective communication enhances your journey through Grand Cayman's sun-soaked paradise, whether you're navigating the island's landscapes, sharing your experiences with loved ones, or immersing yourself in local culture.

50 Communication words and phrases in Grand Cayman Local language

Here are the 50 basic communication words and phrases from Grand Cayman Island, grouped into categories, along with their translations or explanations:

Greetings and Expressions:
1. **Caymanian** - A person from the Cayman Islands.
2. **Yah mon** - A Caribbean expression for agreement or acknowledgment.

43

3. **Cayman Kind** - A term reflecting the friendly and welcoming nature of the locals.

4. **Blessings** - Wishing someone well or expressing gratitude.

5. **Irie** - A Rastafarian term meaning "good" or "everything is alright."

6. **Gimme a bly** - A request for a favor or assistance.

7. **Mi deh yah** - A phrase indicating one's presence or availability.

8. **Wah gwaan** - A Jamaican term meaning "what's going on" or "what's up."

9. **Ya man** - A friendly affirmation, similar to saying "yes" or "okay."

10. **Caymanite smile** - A warm and welcoming smile typical of Caymanians.

11. **Mi soon come** - I will come soon or be there shortly.

12. **Mi cyaan believe it** - I can't believe it.

13. **Mi deh yah fi yuh** - I'm here for you or at your service.

14. **Sweet fuh days** - Exceptionally sweet or enjoyable.

15. **Mi gyal** - Term of endearment for a female friend.

16. **Jus coolin'** - Relaxing or taking it easy.

17. **Mi soon come back** - I will return shortly.

Casual Socializing:

18. **Lime** - A casual social gathering or hanging out with friends.

19. **Dollar wine** - A dance move often seen at social events.

20. **Bredren** - Friends or close associates.

21. **Mi deh pon di rock** - I am on the island (Cayman Islands).

Food and Cuisine:

22. **Conch** - A type of shellfish commonly used in Caymanian cuisine.

23. **Bush tea** - Herbal tea made from locally grown plants.

24. **Rum punch** - A popular local cocktail made with rum and fruit juices.

25. **Ackee and saltfish** - A traditional Caribbean dish.

26. **Mango season** - The time when mangoes are in abundance.

27. **Saltfish and fritters** - Another popular local dish.

28. **Oxtail and rice and peas** - Another popular Caribbean dish.

Nature and Environment:

29. **Cayman breeze** - The refreshing coastal wind that sweeps through the island.

30. **Sea grape** - A type of coastal plant with edible berries.

31. **Island vibes** - The positive and laid-back energy of the Caribbean.

32. **Caymanite** - A local rock or mineral found in the Cayman Islands.

33. **Island time** - Refers to the relaxed and unhurried pace of life in the Caribbean.

34. **Culcha** - Culture or the traditional way of life.

35. **Cayman parrot** - A colorful native bird found in the Cayman Islands.

36. **Sun hot** - The weather is hot and sunny.

37. **Gone to Blue Hole** - A phrase indicating someone has gone swimming or diving.

Travel and Movement:

38. **Mek we go** - Let's go or start moving.

39. **Mi soon come** - I will return shortly.

40. **Deh bout** - Around or nearby.

41. **Mi deh pon di rock** - I am on the island (Cayman Islands).

42. **Lef it deh** - Leave it alone or forget about it.

43. **Gone to Blue Hole** - A phrase indicating someone has gone swimming or diving.

Traditional Wisdom:

44. **Wan wan coco ful baskit** - Literal translation: One one cocoa fills the basket. Patience brings success.

45. **Jus coolin'** - Relaxing or taking it easy.

46. **Mi nuh bizness** - None of my business.

Emergency and Safety:

47. **911** - Emergency contact number for police, fire, and medical assistance.

Expressions of Surprise:

48. **Mi cyaan believe it** - I can't believe it.

Miscellaneous:

49. **Likkle island** - Referring to the small size of the island.

50. **Bush medicine** - Traditional herbal remedies.

These categories capture the essence of communication in Grand Cayman Island, offering a glimpse into the linguistic and cultural richness of this Caribbean paradise.

I am Grateful For The Opportunity To See The World.

Chapter Four: Budget-Friendly Accomodations

Westin Grand Cayman

The Westin Grand Cayman Seven Mile Beach Resort & Spa has everything you need to unwind. Our Grand Cayman, Cayman Islands resort is located on a magnificent oceanfront and provides all you need for a pleasant vacation. Whether you want to enjoy the beach, where you can try your hand at water sports, float in the sparkling waters of our pool, where you can enjoy a refreshing cocktail from our swim-up bar, or pamper yourself at our spa, or work out in our 24-hour WestinWORKOUT Fitness Studio, there's something for everyone.

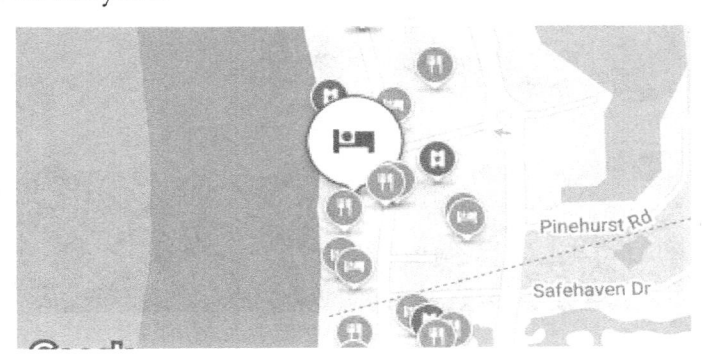

Location: 30620 Seven Mile Beach, Seven Mile Beach KY1-1200 Grand Cayman
Contact: : 009 1 844-631-0595

Grand Cayman Marriott

Relax at the Grand Cayman Marriott. Our Cayman Islands resort is set on the picturesque Seven Mile Beach. Looking for a way to escape the heat of Grand Cayman? Relax at our resort spa, Botanika Union, before indulging in a meal and handmade beverage at one of our chic restaurants.

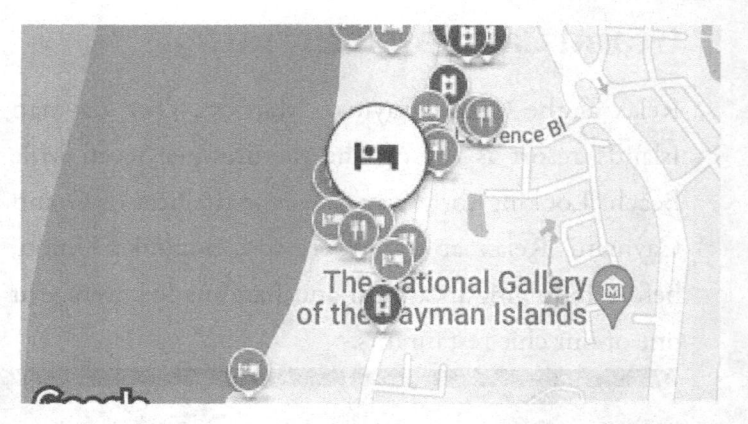

Location: 389 West Bay Road, Seven Mile Beach KY1-1202 Grand Cayman
Contact: 009 1 844-631-0595

Sunshine Suites Resort

Sunshine Suites Resort provides the best in low-cost boutique hotels. We're just a short walk from Grand Cayman's famed Seven Mile Beach with its gorgeous ocean waves and white sand. Enjoy the convenience of our ideal position along Seven Mile Beach, across the street from the 18-hole North Sound Golf Course, and close to a plethora of shops and restaurants. We provide our visitors with high-end rooms, outstanding guest service, and a variety of activities at our sister resort on Seven Mile Beach. Whether you're here for business or pleasure, a warm and welcoming crew greets you!

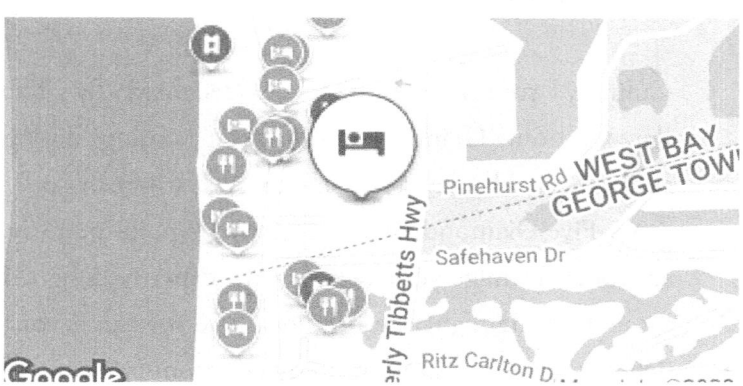

Location: 1465 Esterley Tibbetts Highway, Seven Mile Beach KY1-1201 Grand Cayman

The Ritz-Carlton

At The Ritz-Carlton, Grand Cayman, you may embark on an incredible journey of luxury and refinement. This legendary resort, nestled along the beautiful sands of Seven Mile Beach, offers a unique retreat that perfectly mixes elegance with the natural beauty of the Caribbean.

The Ritz-Carlton, Grand Cayman delivers a world of exquisite elegance and exceptional service with each step inside. The beautiful rooms at the resort redefine luxury living, offering a refuge of comfort and beauty with spectacular views of the turquoise ocean stretching beyond the horizon.

Culinary connoisseurs will be delighted by The Ritz-Carlton, Grand Cayman's outstanding dining experiences. The resort is home to the Caribbean's only AAA-Five Diamond restaurant, bringing cuisine to an art form. Indulge your palette with expertly designed meals that highlight the best local and foreign flavors, delivering an exquisite and unique gastronomic trip.

The Ritz-Carlton, Grand Cayman is a destination for leisure and amusement in addition to its exquisite accommodations and gourmet pleasures. Immerse yourself in the resort's quiet paradise, where luxurious treatments and revitalizing therapies will transport you to a state of happiness. For those seeking adventure, Seven Mile Beach's turquoise seas provide a playground for aquatic sports ranging from snorkeling in bright coral reefs to paddleboarding in the Caribbean heat.

The Ritz-Carlton, Grand Cayman, as a Forbes Five-Star resort, sets the benchmark for quality, ensuring that every minute of your stay is defined by refinement and personalized attention. This resort is a haven where luxury meets the colorful spirit of the Caribbean, whether you're relaxing by the pool, sipping a sunset drink on the beach, or experiencing the excitement of watersports. On this exquisite stretch of paradise, let The Ritz-Carlton, Grand Cayman dazzle you with an unequaled combination of extravagance, natural beauty, and warm hospitality.

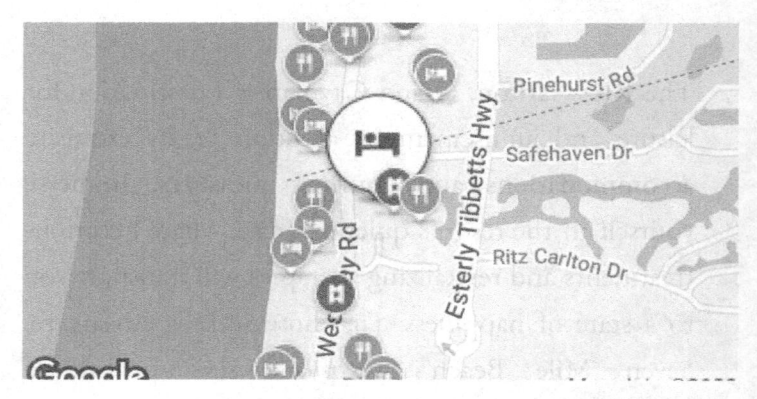

Location: West Bay Rd, Seven Mile Beach KY1-1209 Grand Cayman
Contact: 009 1 844-631-0595

The Locale Hotel

We encourage you to explore Grand Cayman's newest boutique hotel, whether for business or pleasure. The Locale Hotel Grand Cayman is centrally placed along the Seven Mile Beach area. Our central position also provides easy access to George Town and Camana Bay, both of which include restaurants, shopping, and nightlife. Our hotel has 42 contemporary and spacious rooms that are suitable for lone travelers, couples, families, or corporate travelers searching for a convenient spot to work and rest while on business. Our facilities include a pool, Bonfire Urban Kitchen restaurant and craft cocktail bar, and daily breakfast. Friendly, friendly personnel are on hand to deliver a one-of-a-kind vacation experience found only at our boutique hotel.

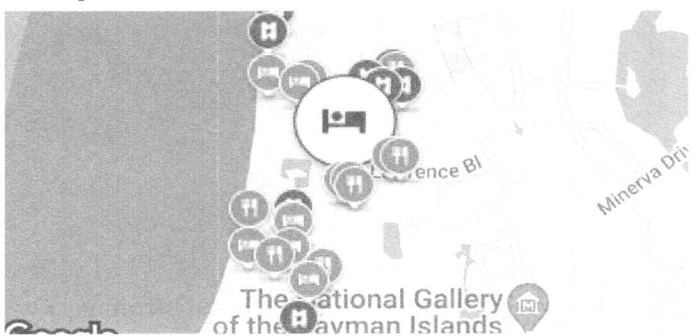

Location: 455 West Bay Road, Seven Mile Beach KY1-1209 Grand Cayman

Contact: 009 1 844-954-3749

Wyndham Reef Resort

Wyndham Reef Resort, an ideal all-beachfront getaway offering an intriguing all-inclusive program on the mesmerizing coastline of Grand Cayman, is a refuge of sun-kissed calm. Your trip into paradise begins with a warm welcome from the white dunes of Grand Cayman, bringing you to a world where crystal-clear seas become your personal playground.

Every room at Wyndham Reef Resort is a beachside retreat, guaranteeing that the charm of the Caribbean is just steps away. Because of the resort's outstanding beachfront position, you can easily move from the luxury of your room to the delights of the seashore. Explore the soft beaches, have some fun, go snorkeling or diving, or simply take in the splendor that awaits you just outside your door.

Wyndham Reef Resort, located in the quiet East End of Grand Cayman, offers a refuge away from the throng, delivering a real tropical escape where tranquility takes center stage. Immerse yourself in the slow pace of island life, where the soft murmur of the waves and the rustling of palm palms provide a soundtrack for relaxation and regeneration.

The resort's dedication to delivering an all-inclusive experience guarantees that your stay is both easy and luxurious. Wyndham Reef Resort caters to your every need, from scrumptious dining options to an assortment of aquatic sports, allowing you to appreciate the spirit of Grand Cayman without a concern in the world.

Whether you're looking for adventure in the undersea wonders, calm contemplation on the beach, or the all-inclusive services that make your stay seamless, Wyndham Reef Resort is a refuge where the beauty of the Caribbean unfolds at your doorstep. Allow the sun-drenched scenery and soothing beat of the waves to create an amazing backdrop for your tropical vacation on Grand Cayman's East End.

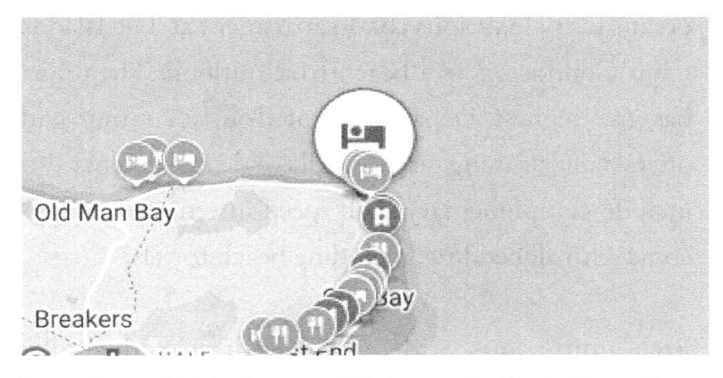

Location: 2221 Queens Highway Collier's Bay, East End KY1-1800 Grand Cayman

The island Club

The Islands Club condominiums on Seven Mile Beach comprise 26 luxury condo apartments, 15 of which are available for rent. These magnificent vacation rental houses provide a wonderful vacation getaway. Whether you want a two, three, or four-bedroom apartment, each one has its own private patio or balcony that overlooks Seven Mile Beach. Many nice restaurants, duty-free stores, nightclubs, golf courses, a modern grocery store, water sports, and other activities are easily accessible.

Large Casuarina trees flank the beach, offering plenty of shade while you relax on a lounge chair near the ocean. Every luxurious condo apartment at The Islands Club Condos offers a beachfront outlook. The resort has the highest Department of Tourism rating and offers daily cleaning services. All condo apartments also include complimentary high-speed internet access and come with all bedding, including beach towels.

Each unit comes with a washer/dryer and a fully equipped kitchen. A fitness facility and a lighted tennis court are among the on-site attractions. Each unit comes equipped with central air conditioning, telephones, and cable television. Select apartments provide free long-distance calling. Chef services and catering are also offered, as are cribs, high chairs, and babysitter services.

The Islands Club Condos, located on the greatest stretch of Seven Mile Beach, includes towering Casuarina trees that give plenty of shade. Even when completely booked, visitors will never feel cramped on the beach. The Islands Club Condos in Grand Cayman consistently surpass expectations and have long been considered as one of the island's premier beachfront rental properties. Guests come year after year, making it their home under the sun. Come enjoy our tiny corner of heaven!

63

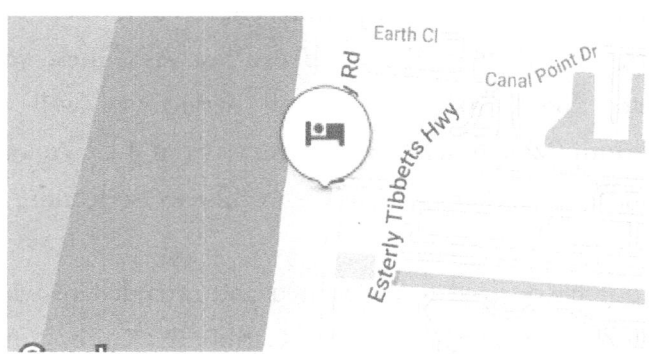

Location: 809 West Bay Road, 7 Mile Beach, Grand, Seven Mile Beach KY1-1203 Grand Cayman

The Caribbean Club

The Caribbean Club, located in the center of Seven Mile Beach, is a beacon of luxury, providing luxurious 1-3 bedroom villas and suites for an unforgettable visit. Each suite is a luxurious sanctuary with a large living area that is seamlessly connected to a fully equipped gourmet kitchen. Step onto the lovely balcony, which is furnished with a dining table and lounge chairs, and be fascinated by the magnificent views of Seven Mile Beach.

The oceanfront homes, constructed straight onto the white dunes, are a masterpiece for those seeking the pinnacle of beachside life. These luxurious suites have wrap-around terraces with direct access to the beach or stunning views of the Caribbean Sea. As a guest, you can expect individual beach service as well as scrumptious lunches and dinners from LUCA, our onsite restaurant that symbolizes culinary perfection.

Your every need is anticipated and attended to with greatest accuracy at the Caribbean Club. Our commitment to luxury guarantees that your stay is nothing short of amazing, whether you're savoring a gourmet dinner, enjoying the beachside experience, or resting in the vast comfort of your suite. Immerse yourself in the realm of refinement at the Caribbean Club, where every detail is meant to take your Seven Mile Beach escape to the peak of enjoyment.

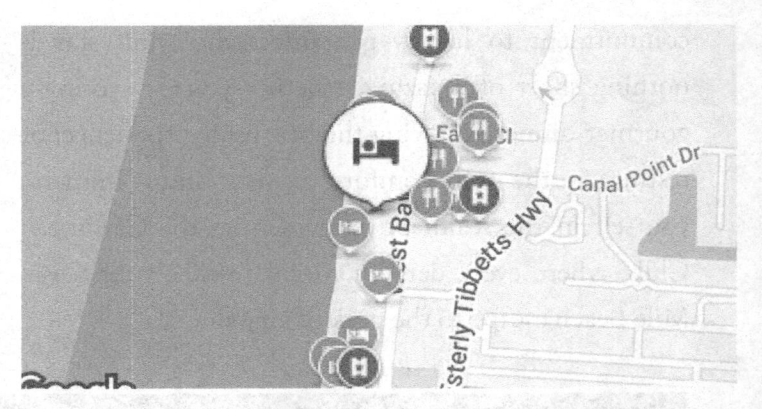

Location: 871 West Bay Road, Seven Mile Beach KY1-1200 Grand Cayman
Contact: 009 1 844-454-4126

The Grand Cayman Resort

The Grand Caymanian Resort is located on the North Sound of Grand Cayman and shares amenities with the Holiday Inn Resort. It's the perfect location for business retreats, weddings, and other special events. Guests may relax on the poolside covered patio and beachfront pavilion while taking in the calm surroundings.

The resort provides a variety of recreational activities, such as working out at the on-site Fitness Center, playing pickleball, and having a leisurely stroll around the local golf course. The Driftwood Bar & Grill offers delectable drinks and global cuisine, ensuring a memorable dining experience.

Nestled in one of the world's most magnificent settings, the hotel is surrounded by palm palms, ocean views, and coastal breezes. It's the only resort on the North Sound Caribbean Sea, and the sea-side pool provides stunning views of sunrise.

The hotel offers ironing boards and irons, as well as accommodations with a microwave and small refrigerator or a full kitchen, dining area, and living room. Concierge services, dry cleaning, coin laundry, and room service are among the amenities offered. Guests may also visit the on-site DiveTech Dive shop and use the business center.

The resort offers a number of eating options, including the Driftwood Bar & Grill and Pool Bar. Other amenities include complimentary pickleball on-site, complimentary beach towels and chairs, and 24-hour access to the on-site health center. Guests may also enjoy the freshwater pool, which has a sun deck, beach annexes, and cabanas.

The Grand Caymanian Resort, with its assortment of services and magnificent settings, provides guests with an amazing vacation in paradise.

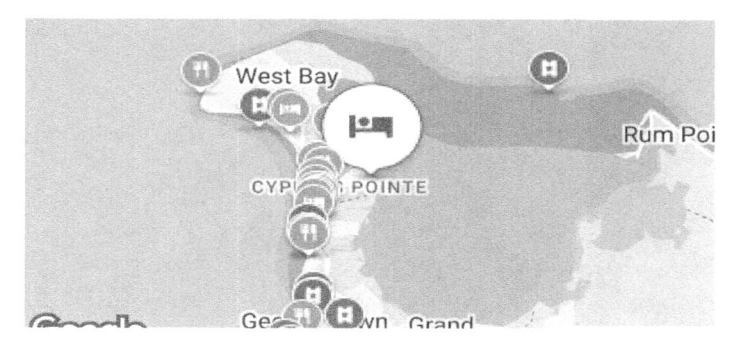

Location: 276 Crighton Drive, West Bay KY1-1206 Grand Cayman
Contact: 009 1 855-337-0101

Villas of The Galleon

Located in the heart of Seven Mile Beach, close to grocery/liquor stores, a few outstanding restaurants, and watersports. Villas with one, two, or three bedrooms with views of the Caribbean Sea are available. Fully equipped with central air conditioning, free Wi-Fi, and on-site management, the apartments have all been freshly refurbished, modernized, and are typically designed with all of your home's comforts. Daily housekeeping is given, as well as shade trees, beach umbrellas, lounge chairs, and beach towels. What more could you want from a vacation? We wish you could be here.

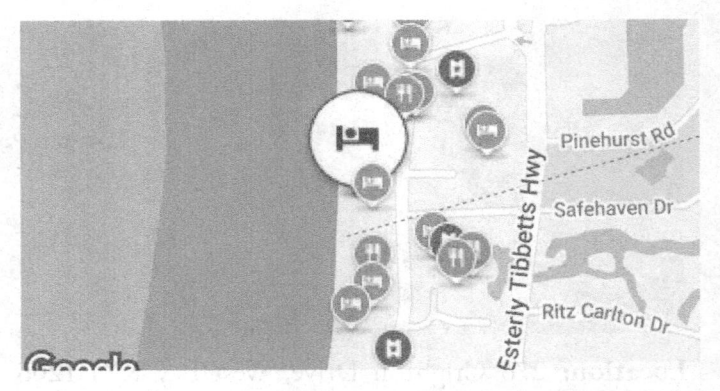

Location: 1083 West Bay Road, Seven Mile Beach KY1-1109 Grand Cayman
Contact: 009 1 866-665-4696

Chapter Five: Must Visit Attractions

Hell

Hell" is situated at 22 Hell Road, West Bay, Grand Cayman

A strange and enchanting site greets travelers on the whimsically called Grand Cayman island – the interesting area known as "Hell." Despite its frightening reputation, Hell is a geological wonder that invites visitors to view a one-of-a-kind environment sculpted by nature's forces over millions of years.

The harsh and unearthly limestone structures that dominate the area give Hell its name. Visitors to Hell are welcomed with jagged black limestone rocks, producing an almost bizarre environment in sharp contrast to Grand Cayman's beautiful tropical surroundings. These structures, produced by the erosion of old coral reefs, add to the area's enchantment.

Visitors can stroll through the Hell Post Office upon arrival, a peculiar attraction that allows them to mail postcards postmarked from "Hell" to friends and family. Souvenirs are available in the Hell gift store, allowing visitors to take a piece of this geological anomaly home with them.

While Hell isn't your typical beach location, its unusual geological characteristics and the opportunity to explore this natural marvel make it a worthy trip for anyone looking to venture beyond the sun-kissed shoreline. A journey to Hell offers an unearthly experience, where nature's powers have built a genuinely one-of-a-kind and spectacular site on Grand Cayman island.

Porto di Georgetown (Port of George Town)

The Porto di Georgetown, or Port of George Town, on Grand Cayman's western shore, emerges as a dynamic focal point and the principal maritime entry to the island's charms. This lively harbor, located at 19.2894° N latitude and 81.3857° W longitude, not only serves as an important port of entry for cruise ships but also embodies Grand Cayman's energetic personality.

The colorful atmosphere quickly captivates guests as they stroll into the Porto di Georgetown coastline. Colorful structures provide a stunning panorama, representing the vibrant junction of local life and foreign tourism. This beachfront enclave is a visual feast that captures the island's vivacious energy.

The duty-free stores, boutiques, and local markets that dominate the port area will thrill shoppers. Porto di Georgetown delivers a variety and enjoyable shopping experience for guests, ranging from high-end items to genuinely produced Caymanian treasures.

Culinary connoisseurs may enjoy waterfront dining at the port's various restaurants and cafés. Patrons may enjoy fresh seafood or foreign cuisine while taking in panoramic views of the Caribbean Sea.

Porto di Georgetown also acts as a springboard to cultural discovery. Historic monuments, museums, and landmarks are all within walking distance, encouraging tourists to dig into Grand Cayman's rich legacy. Porto di Georgetown, as a marine jewel and cultural crossroads, invites visitors to immerse themselves in the colorful spirit of this Caribbean paradise.

Cayman Crystal Caves

Drops of water and the passage of time show the distinct rainforest habitat that gave origin to the Cayman Crystal Caves. The forest and caves are home to a diverse range of flora and animals, including strangler fig trees, air plants, parrots, and bats.

The Cayman Crystal Caves have been formed over millions of years. Fossilized shells and signs of animal life within the caverns suggest that the mass around the caves was once buried beneath the sea. As sea levels rose and land arose, water erosion created chambers, which eventually became caves.

Rainwater pouring through the limestone roof of the caverns caused calcium deposits, resulting in the formation of magnificent stalagmite and stalactite crystal formations within the chambers. These tunnels continue to evolve even now.

The formation of stalagmites and stalactites happens when rainfall, somewhat acidic after passing through adjacent plants and organic material, dissolves a portion of the limestone ceiling. The dissolved calcium is subsequently redeposited in microscopic layers, resulting in the crystal forms throughout time.

Centuries ago, pirates used these tunnels as hideouts and weather shelters. As the Cayman Islands' population grew, the surrounding plains were used for farming, and the caverns were mined for fertilizer rich in bat guano, as some caves were home to bats.

In recent decades, farming has declined as people turn to more profitable businesses like as tourism and finance. In the early 1990s, Christian and Ole Sorensen surveyed all of the Cayman Islands' caverns and began conversations with the government about building a cave attraction based on their successful experience with Harrison's caverns in Barbados.

After two decades of labor, including the acquisition of adjacent lands and the development of access ways, the crystal caves of Old Man Bay emerged as a really spectacular destination. Ergun Berksoy and the Berksoy family, with their significant tourism industry experience, joined the Sorensen family to complete Cayman's newest and most exciting tourist attraction.

Seven Mile Beach

If you're searching for a tropical holiday, try staying at a seaside resort on Seven Mile Beach—sipping fresh coconut juice while bathing in the Caribbean heat will quickly soothe you. Swim in the warm, clear water or ride a banana boat for an exciting trip. Snorkel in the coral reefs to see stingrays and turtles, among other marine species.

The northern end of this busy section is considered the greatest. Dining options range from food trucks to gourmet dining establishments, all of which are within walking distance of one another.

Stingray City

Stingray City emerges as a unique and magical location, catching the hearts of travelers seeking an unforgettable marine adventure in the cerulean seas of Grand Cayman. This unique sandbar in Grand Cayman's North Sound is recognized as a natural sanctuary where tourists may interact with and marvel at the beautiful Southern Stingrays.

The charm of Stingray City rests in its shallow, crystal-clear waters, which make it a great location for an immersive and unique experience with these gorgeous creatures. The friendly Southern Stingrays smoothly glide through the water, producing a stunning show for snorkelers and divers alike.

To get up close and personal with the stingrays, visitors may wade into the shallow sandbar or go on guided snorkeling and diving trips. The delicate nature of these marine treasures allows for once-in-a-lifetime experiences, with visitors able to touch, feed, and even pose for photographs with the stingrays while under the cautious eye of trained rangers.

Stingray City is more than just a tourist attraction for marine aficionados; it is a living monument to the coexistence of humans and animals. The excitement of being in the presence of these friendly creatures in the middle of shimmering waterways generates memories that last long after the excursion is over. Stingray City is an aquatic paradise for those looking for a unique combination of adventure and marine wonder, encouraging tourists to delve into the beauty and elegance of Grand Cayman's undersea universe.

Queen Elizabeth II Botanic Park

The Queen Elizabeth II Botanic Park, nestled in the calm landscapes of Grand Cayman, is a horticultural marvel, encouraging visitors to discover the rich tapestry of flora and fauna that characterizes the Caribbean's natural beauty. This 65-acre botanical park on the island's north side is a paradise for nature enthusiasts and those looking for a peaceful vacation.

Visitors will meet a vast mix of indigenous and exotic plant species as they wander around the park's verdant walkways, from vivid orchids and bromeliads to towering palms and fragrant blossoms. The Woodland Trail, a shaded promenade through the park's core, offers a serene stroll, while the Floral Color Garden bursts with vivid colors, creating a beautiful symphony.

The fascinating Blue Iguana Habitat, a conservation area dedicated to the protection of the endangered Grand Cayman Blue Iguana, is the showpiece of the Queen Elizabeth II Botanic Park. Visitors may see these wonderful species in their native environment, which contributes to the park's dedication to biodiversity protection.

The Heritage Garden highlights traditional Caymanian plants, providing a look into the island's rich botanical heritage for visitors seeking cultural insights. The tranquil lake, blossoming with water lilies, provides a beautiful setting for rest and introspection.

The Queen Elizabeth II Botanic Park promises a mesmerizing excursion into Grand Cayman's natural beauties, whether wandering around the complex gardens, birding, or engaging in guided tours. It's a haven where the brilliant colors and smells of the Caribbean's different ecosystems come to life, encouraging visitors to interact with the island's botanical history in a serene and natural environment.

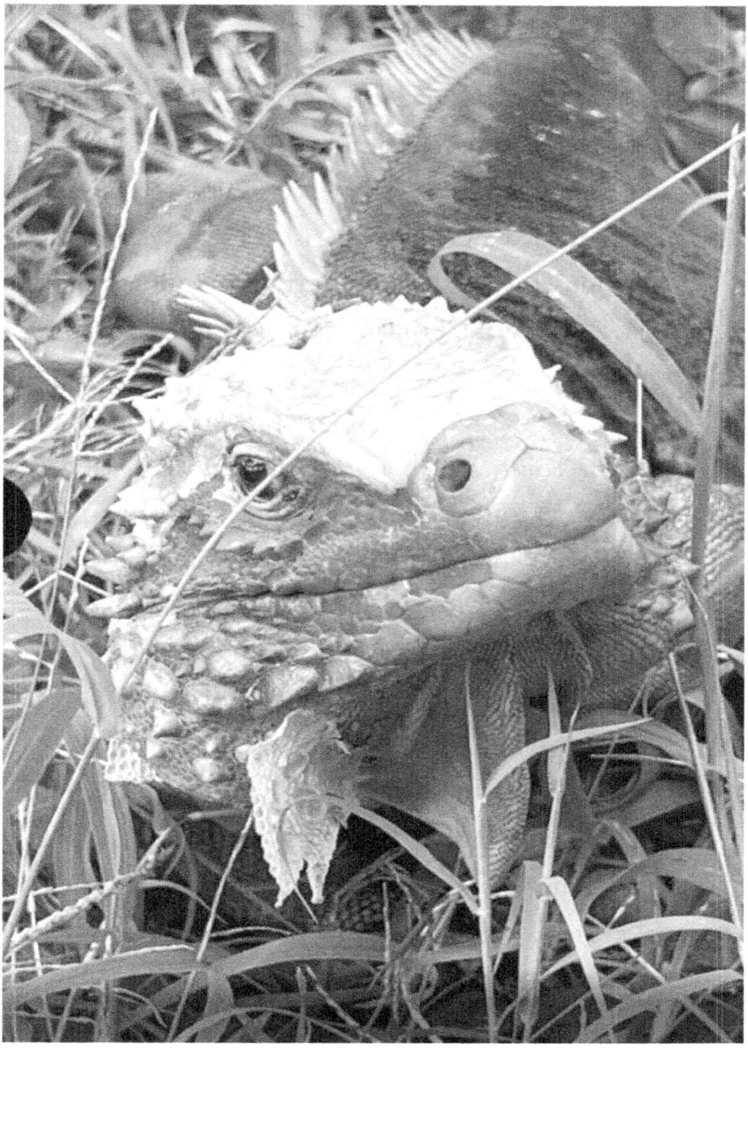

Starfish Point

Starfish Point, located on Grand Cayman's northern coast, has captured the hearts of travelers seeking a calm and romantic seaside experience. This lovely stretch of beach, tucked away from the island's hustle and bustle, is famous for its shallow, crystal-clear waters and the chance to see the brilliant and distinctive cushion sea stars.

Starfish Point, which is accessible by both land and water, is a monument to Grand Cayman's natural splendor. The gentle, sandy beach provides a wonderful backdrop for relaxation and exploration, making it an ideal location for families, nature lovers, and those seeking a calm vacation.

The quantity of cushion sea stars that adorn the shallows at Starfish Point is, of course, the major attraction. These intriguing animals, which range in color from vivid orange to deep red, form a living mosaic under the water's surface. Visitors are invited to walk into the mild waves and get up close and personal with these aquatic treasures while maintaining the delicate balance of their natural environment.

Beyond the sea stars, the beach provides panoramic views of the Caribbean Sea and the distant horizon, making it an idyllic setting for a day of coastal solitude. The ride to Starfish Point by boat is a picturesque excursion that reveals Grand Cayman's coastline beauty.

Starfish Point is more than a destination; it's a haven where the rhythm of the waves, the soothing caress of the sea wind, and the vivid colors of marine life come together to create a unique seaside experience on Grand Cayman's coastlines.

Cemetery Beach and Reef

Cemetery Beach and Reef, located on Grand Cayman's western shore, is a hidden haven for travelers looking for a tranquil vacation and spectacular underwater excursions. This lovely stretch of coastline, located in the West Bay region, with a calm beach and an appealing coral that draws snorkelers and divers alike. This West Bay treasure is easily accessible, providing a calm alternative to the island's more busy beaches.

The beach's unusual name comes from a neighboring cemetery, providing a fascinating historical element to the natural beauty that it reveals. Cemetery Beach is well-known for its immaculate white beaches and peaceful, crystal-clear seas, making it a perfect site for leisure as well as exploration.

The neighboring Cemetery Reef offers a lively marine ecology overflowing with beautiful coral formations and a variety of tropical fish for underwater aficionados. Snorkelers may readily access the reef from the beach, immersing themselves in an enthralling underwater environment only feet away.

Cemetery Beach and Reef, with its relaxed atmosphere and enthralling marine life, is an ideal destination for visitors wishing to unwind and discover the delights of Grand Cayman's coastal treasures. Visitors will find a genuine sanctuary for nature lovers in this West Bay gem, whether lounging in the sun on the sandy sands or finding the brilliant coral beneath the waves.

Cayman Turtle Centre

The Cayman Turtle Conservation and Education Centre is more than just a sea turtle rescue center; it's also a hub of wild island fun and a cutting-edge wildlife conservation experience. Visitors to this one-of-a-kind facility may not only observe the magnificence of Green sea turtles, but also participate in a variety of interesting activities that help to marine conservation.

Immerse yourself in the conservation quest by swimming among lively juvenile turtles and admiring majestic Green sea turtles. Experience the excitement of seeing small hatchlings emerge from their nests, demonstrating the center's successful efforts to reduce poaching and increase the wild sea turtle population.

Aside from turtle interactions, the facility provides a variety of entertaining activities. Take a ride down the Turtle Twister waterslide, marvel at the soaring rainbows in the Butterfly House and Free Flight Aviary, and go into the mysterious realm of Predator Reef.

Importantly, the Cayman Turtle protection and Education Centre is dedicated to educating tourists and encouraging them to become champions for sea turtle protection. Learn about the center's creative ways, the obstacles that sea turtles confront, and how you can help to conserve these beautiful creatures. It's more than just a visit; it's an opportunity to have fun, learn about sea turtles, and actively contribute to their conservation in the Caribbean.

Kittiwake Shipwreck & Artificial Reef

The Kittiwake Shipwreck & Artificial Reef is a mesmerizing underwater habitat off the coast of Grand Cayman that draws both seasoned divers and curious snorkelers. This sunken warship, located in the seas off Seven Mile Beach, acts as a unique marine environment, providing tourists with an exciting underwater journey.

The Kittiwake Shipwreck's precise coordinates are around 19.3610° N latitude and 81.3969° W longitude. This cleverly designed artificial reef provides a home for aquatic life while providing underwater aficionados with a memorable experience.

The Kittiwake, a former United States Navy submarine rescue vessel, was intentionally sunk in 2011 to serve as an artificial reef and marine sanctuary. The wreckage, which is now at a depth accessible to both divers and snorkelers, exemplifies a captivating marriage of nautical history and marine conservation.

Divers may explore the ship's labyrinthine compartments and passages, where they will find brilliant coral formations and a plethora of aquatic life. Snorkelers may see the massive structure beneath them and the diverse marine ecology living in and around the sunken warship from the surface.

The Kittiwake Shipwreck & Artificial Reef exemplifies Grand Cayman's dedication to marine conservation and adventure tourism. It's more than simply a diving site; it's a live example of the symbiotic interaction that exists between the undersea ecosystem and those who wish to explore its depths. It promises tourists an immersive and instructive contact with the Caribbean's underwater treasures.

92

Chapter Six: Grand Cayman Cultural Insights

Embracing Grand Cayman Culture and traditions

Grand Cayman, the Cayman Islands' crown gem, is a mesmerizing canvas painted with a rich tapestry of cultural traditions, genuine hospitality, and a profound connection to the Caribbean way of life. Understanding the cultural subtleties of this lovely island enriches the visitor's experience, providing a look into Grand Cayman's character.

1. **Culinary Delights: A Flavor Fusion

The dynamic and diversified food scene on Grand Cayman is at the heart of the island's cultural character. The native cuisine is a celebration of tastes and skills, influenced by a combination of African, European, and Caribbean traditions. Visitors are welcome to go on a culinary adventure that symbolizes the island's history and the wealth of its surrounding oceans, from the world-famous conch dishes to the delectable jerk chicken. Exploring local markets, like the lively Farmers' Market in George Town, allows you to sample fresh vegetables and connect with the island's gastronomic pulse.

2. **Music and Dance: The Caribbean Rhythms**

Grand Cayman's essence is infused with music and dance, which mimic the exuberant rhythms of the Caribbean. The island comes alive with the sounds of native performers, from energetic soca beats to beautiful reggae tunes. Visitors may feel the excitement of ancient dance forms influenced by African and European influences, such as quadrille. Attending local festivals and events puts you in the front row for exciting cultural performances that highlight the island's musical diversity and the kindness of its inhabitants.

3. **Fishing and Maritime Heritage: Seafaring Traditions**

Caymanians' livelihoods and cultural identities have been shaped by the water, which has been a constant companion throughout their life. The historic catboat races, in which elegant vessels negotiate the blue seas with expert precision, highlight Grand Cayman's maritime legacy. Fishing is still a popular pastime, and tourists may see fisherman bringing in their daily harvest in docks such as George Town's Fish Market. Engaging with residents and learning about their maritime traditions gives you a better understanding of the island's connection to the water.

4. **Island Time: Adopting a Slower Pace

Grand Cayman works on a distinct idea known as "island time," which encourages both inhabitants and visitors to live at a slower pace, relishing the moments without the bustle of the outside world. Island time is more than simply a timetable; it's a way of life that invites everyone to embrace the natural beauty and simple pleasures that Grand Cayman has to offer.

5. **Handcrafted Treasures from Cayman

Artisanal crafts serve an important part in the preservation of Caymanian customs. Visit local markets and galleries to find homemade gifts ranging from delicate thatch work to brilliant Caymanite jewelry. Engaging with local artists reveals the talent and passion necessary to make these one-of-a-kind creations, each of which tells a narrative about the island's cultural past.

6. **Religious Diversity: Coexistence in Peace

Grand Cayman is a religious melting pot, with numerous religions coexisting together. Churches of many religions dot the landscape, and tourists are encouraged to join services and festivals to experience the island's spiritual side. The harmony in diversity reflects the Caymanian mentality, which values religious freedom and tolerance.

7. **National Heroes and Celebrations: Remembering the Past

Grand Cayman honors its national heroes, those who have played important roles in defining the island's history and culture. National Heroes Day and the Queen's Birthday Parade are more than just festivities; they are displays of national pride and appreciation for people who have contributed to the Cayman Islands' growth.

Grand Cayman's cultural knowledge is essentially a tapestry of smells, sounds, customs, and friendliness. Visitors are invited to participate in the native way of life rather than merely observe it, establishing a deeper connection with the genuine essence of this Caribbean paradise. The warmth of Caymanian culture remains in the hearts of those who are lucky enough to experience its embrace as the sun sets over Seven Mile Beach.

Events and festivals

Grand Cayman, a Caribbean treasure, captivates not only with its beautiful beaches and turquoise oceans, but also with a calendar of exciting festivals and events that highlight the island's rich cultural legacy and energetic character. Here's a guide to the festivals and events that guarantee a memorable voyage into Caribbean celebration for tourists seeking to immerse themselves in the spirit of Grand Cayman.

Swashbuckling Extravaganza

Time: November (every year)

Location: All across Grand Cayman

Adventurers, ahoy! Set sail for Grand Cayman in November to participate in the exciting Pirates Week Festival, a week-long celebration that transforms the island into a bustling pirate paradise. The celebration embodies the essence of nautical history and seafaring customs and is often hosted in the center of George Town and several sites across Grand Cayman.

Immerse yourself in the celebrations by seeing parades of buccaneers, street dances to exciting Caribbean rhythms, and fake pirate attacks along the coastlines. A treasure trove of events awaits families, including costume contests, historical reenactments, and magnificent fireworks displays that up the night sky.

Pirates Week is more than just a party; it's a cultural immersion into the island's maritime history. Join the residents and guests in dressing up in pirate garb, dancing to the beat of steel drums, and enjoying in the camaraderie that distinguishes this swashbuckling event. Pirates Week is a dynamic presentation of Grand Cayman's passionate community and its determination to preserve the island's seafaring traditions, from the colorful costumes to the enthralling spectacles.

Carnival at Batabano

Time: May (every year)

Location: George Town, Grand Cayman
The brilliant colors of the Caribbean come to life in May at the Batabano Carnival in George Town, Grand Cayman. This vibrant carnival has masquerade bands,

spectacular costumes, and irresistible dance rhythms that fill the streets with color and excitement.

Join the march of revelers through George Town, displaying artistic expressions that pay respect to the island's rich cultural variety. The flamboyant outfits, influenced by Caribbean customs, weave a colorful tapestry of inventiveness. Visitors are urged to dress up and participate in the rhythmic dance processions, feeling the throbbing rhythms of Caribbean drums and immersing themselves in the island's festive atmosphere.

The Batabano Carnival exemplifies Grand Cayman's dedication to conserving and promoting its unique history. This May event promises an exciting voyage into the heart of Caribbean celebration for anyone looking for an authentic and colorful cultural experience.

A Gastronomic Extravaganza on Cayman

Time: January (every year)
Locations: Various locations in Grand Cayman

In January, treat your taste buds to the Cayman Cookout, a gastronomic event that enriches Grand Cayman's culinary landscape. This yearly event brings together famous chefs, sommeliers, and food connoisseurs from all over the world for a series of gourmet experiences set against the stunning scenery of the Caribbean.

Explore Grand Cayman's various cuisines through seaside barbecues, special dinners, and culinary demonstrations that highlight the island's dedication to farm-to-table quality. Attendees will be able to sample fresh, locally sourced ingredients and interact with the chefs behind each dish.

The Cayman Cookout is more than simply a food festival; it's also a celebration of the island's culinary tradition and inventiveness. Whether you're a seasoned gourmet or simply admire the artistry of good dining, this event provides a one-of-a-kind opportunity to immerse yourself in the tastes of Grand Cayman while socializing with other foodies.

Cayman Islands Carnival

Time: May (every year)
Location: George Town, Grand Cayman

During the Cayman Islands Carnival in May, the Cayman Islands come alive with the exciting sounds of soca, reggae, and calypso. This spectacular event is a blend of music, dancing, and cultural expression that transforms George Town's streets into a colorful and rhythmic extravaganza.

Participate in the exciting parades with costumed dancers, enjoy the pounding beats of Caribbean music, and immerse yourself in the carnival mood that characterizes this dynamic celebration. The streets are transformed into a dance floor as residents and visitors alike gather together to celebrate the Cayman Islands' rich cultural variety.

Participate in the dancing processions, dress brightly, and revel in the contagious enthusiasm of the Cayman Islands Carnival. This vibrant festival not only highlights the island's cultural richness, but also encourages everyone to join in on the rhythmic celebration that reverberates through Grand Cayman's heart.

CayFilm

Time: Annually
Locations: Various locations in Grand Cayman

CayFilm, the Cayman International Film Festival, provides a cinematic celebration against the gorgeous background of Grand Cayman for film aficionados and creatives. This yearly festival features a varied selection of local and international films, giving artists a platform to share their work with the globe.

CayFilm offers screenings, seminars, panel discussions, and opportunities to engage with industry experts at several venues around the island. This festival offers a unique cultural experience that merges the magic of storytelling with the natural beauty of Grand Cayman, whether you're a filmmaker, a film aficionado, or someone wanting to explore the world of cinema.

Discover Caribbean cinema's artistry and originality while basking in the warmth of Caribbean hospitality. CayFilm is more than simply a film festival; it's an investigation of narrative, cultural interaction, and the power of cinematic arts in the Caribbean's heart.

Cayman Arts Festival

Time: Annually

Locations: Various locations in Grand Cayman

The Cayman Arts Festival is an annual event that brings together local and international artists to display their abilities in music, dance, and the performing arts for people who enjoy the arts. This cultural festival, which takes place at several sites around Grand Cayman, serves as a forum for artistic expression and cultural interaction.

Concerts, recitals, dance performances, and theatrical plays of all genres and styles are available to audiences. The festival not only showcases Caymanian artists' talent, but also welcomes foreign performers to share their craft with the local community and tourists.

Whether you're a music lover, a dancer, or someone looking for a cultural experience, the Cayman Arts Festival presents a symphony of performances that engage the senses and honor Grand Cayman's artistic soul.

Cayman's National Heroes Day

Time: January (every year)
Location: George Town, Grand Cayman

National Heroes Day, observed in January, honors those who have made outstanding contributions to the development and culture of the Cayman Islands. The festival, which takes place in George Town, Cayman, features a spectacular ceremony, parades, and cultural acts that highlight the island's patriotic spirit and national pride.

Visitors may experience bright displays of Caymanian heritage, participate in traditional rites, and interact with the local community as they join together to remember their national heroes on National Heroes Day. It's a chance to learn about the island's history, cultural legacy, and the people who have played important roles in establishing Caymanian identity.

During National Heroes Day, join the locals in celebrating, experiencing the warmth of Caymanian hospitality, and paying respect to people who have made an indelible impact on the cultural landscape of Grand Cayman.

In essence, these festivals and events are more than just celebrations; they are portals into Grand Cayman's vivid spirit. Whether it's the swashbuckling antics of Pirates Week, the rhythmic revelry of Batabano Carnival, or the gourmet pleasures of Cayman Cookout, each event provides a distinct lens through which visitors may experience Grand Cayman's cultural diversity and vivacity. Consider aligning your vacation with one of these festivals when you plan your trip to add an added layer of cultural immersion to your Caribbean break.

Tips for Attending Grand Cayman Events and Festivals

Attending events and festivals in Grand Cayman offers a vibrant and enriching experience, providing insights into the local culture, traditions, and community spirit. Here are some tips to make the most of your time at these gatherings:

1. **Plan Ahead:** Research upcoming events and festivals in Grand Cayman to ensure you don't miss out on any exciting happenings during your visit. Check local event calendars, tourism websites, and social media channels for information on dates, locations, and activities.

2. **Pack Accordingly**: Consider the nature of the event and pack appropriate attire and essentials. For beach festivals, bring sunscreen, hats, and swimsuits. If attending evening events, opt for light layers as temperatures may cool down.

3. **Arrive Early**: To avoid crowds and secure prime viewing spots, arrive early to popular events and festivals. This allows you to explore the venue, get acquainted with the surroundings, and soak in the atmosphere before the festivities begin.

4. **Respect Local Customs**: Familiarize yourself with local customs and etiquette to show respect for the host community. Be mindful of cultural sensitivities, dress modestly when appropriate, and follow any guidelines or rules set by event organizers.

5. **Stay Hydrated and Energized**: Grand Cayman's events and festivals can be lively and energetic affairs, so remember to stay hydrated by drinking plenty of water throughout the day. Snack on local treats to keep your energy levels up and sample the delicious cuisine offered at food stalls and vendors.

6. **Embrace the Music and Dance**: Many events in Grand Cayman feature live music, traditional dance performances, and cultural entertainment. Immerse yourself in the sounds and rhythms of local music, and don't be afraid to join in the dancing and celebration.

7. **Engage with Locals**: Strike up conversations with locals and fellow attendees to learn more about the event, its significance, and the traditions behind it. Grand Cayman residents are known for their warmth and hospitality, so don't hesitate to connect with them and make new friends.

8. **Capture Memories**: Bring a camera or smartphone to capture memorable moments and document your experiences at Grand Cayman events and festivals. Share your photos and stories with friends and family to spread the joy and excitement of your travels.

By following these tips, you can fully immerse yourself in the vibrant cultural tapestry of Grand Cayman's events and festivals, creating unforgettable memories and forging connections with the local community.

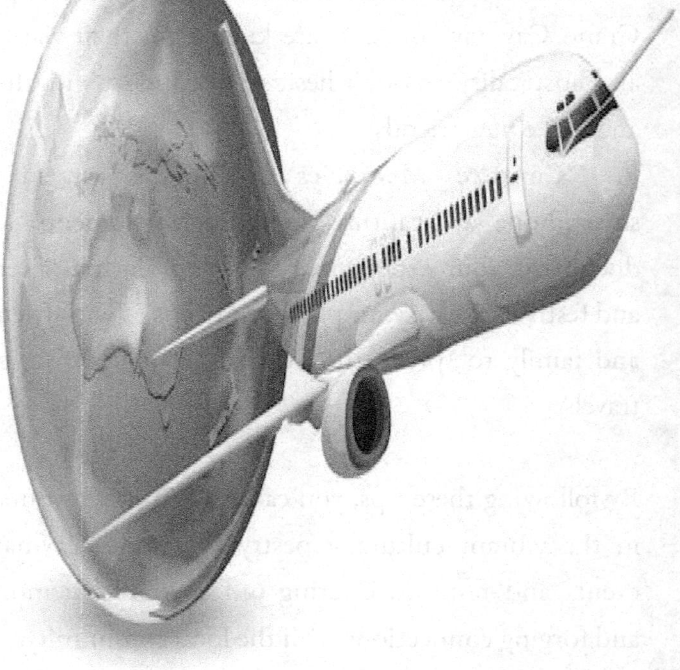

Chapter Seven: Grand Cayman Culinary Delight

Grand Cayman Cafes and Restaurants

Beyond its gorgeous beaches and pristine oceans, Grand Cayman is a gastronomic paradise that draws foodies from all over the world. The eating scene on the island is a blend of tastes, drawing inspiration from Caribbean, European, and international cuisines. Here's a guide to some of Grand Cayman's trendiest cafés and restaurants that promise to tickle taste buds and enrich the eating experience for guests looking for a gourmet voyage.

1. **Calypso Grill: Fresh Seafood and Coastal Elegance

Calypso Grill, located on the waterfront at Morgan's Harbour, embodies coastal elegance and culinary quality. With breathtaking views of the Caribbean Sea, this stylish restaurant embodies the essence of Grand Cayman's marine tradition. Executive Chef George Fowler's menu features a selection of fresh seafood, from the catch of the day to specialty dishes like the Cayman Bouillabaisse. The open-air atmosphere, along with the superb service, produces a dining experience that combines refinement with the relaxed charm of island living.

2. **Eric Ripert's Blue: Michelin-Starred Perfection

Blue by Eric Ripert at The Ritz-Carlton, Grand Cayman is a culinary marvel for those looking for a dining experience that exceeds expectations. This Michelin-starred restaurant, created by famed Chef Eric Ripert, serves a meal inspired by the riches of the sea. The magnificent setting, enhanced by ocean vistas, sets the stage for an excellent trip through seafood delights. From the trademark Blue Lobster to the exquisite sashimi options, each dish is a piece of beauty that shows Chef Ripert's culinary genius.

3. **Cayman Coffee Club: An Island Caffeine Haven

Cayman Coffee Club in George Town is a stylish café that captivates residents and visitors alike for a pleasant coffee fix and a taste of island charm. This quaint institution provides a friendly environment in which coffee aficionados may sample expertly prepared beans originating from all around the world. Whether you like a basic espresso or a uniquely prepared latte, the baristas at Cayman Coffee Club take pleasure in providing an aromatic and artisanal coffee experience. For a nice respite from your island adventure, pair your coffee with a tasty pastry or a small snack.

4. **The Brasserie: Farm-to-Table Gourmet

The Brasserie, located in the center of GeorgeTown, is a symbol of farm-to-table quality on Grand Cayman. This hip restaurant not only highlights the island's culinary skills, but also demonstrates a dedication to sustainability with its on-site garden and farm. Chef Dean Max's cuisine embraces local tastes with meals made from fresh, organic ingredients. Each item at The Brasserie, from the Black Angus Beef Carpaccio to the colorful heirloom tomato salads, is a monument to the island's agricultural richness and the chefs' culinary talent.

5. **Morgan's: Caribbean-Inspired Waterfront Dining

Morgan's at the Cayman Islands Yacht Club, perched on the edge of the North Sound, provides a refined waterfront dining experience blended with Caribbean flare. Surrounded by turquoise oceans and luxurious boats, the restaurant sets the tone for an elite gastronomic excursion. Chef Jonathan Rivard has created a meal that combines foreign and local tastes. Guests may savor meals like Lobster and Shrimp Risotto or Pan-Seared Grouper while taking in the spectacular views of the marina.

6. **Anchor & Den: International Culinary Playground

Anchor & Den is a dynamic culinary playground located within the Grand Cayman Marriott Beach Resort that flawlessly integrates global influences with indigenous ingredients. This modern restaurant serves a diversified cuisine that appeals to a wide range of tastes, from tasty sushi rolls to delectable Caribbean-inspired meals. The open and elegant environment, along with live music, produces a dynamic atmosphere that is ideal for both casual meals and special events. Guests may also peruse the inventive drink menu, which features handmade cocktails made with accuracy and originality.

7. **Agua: Latin Flavors in a Chic Environment

Agua at Camana Bay is a must-visit site for Latin American-inspired food in a trendy setting. This modern restaurant mixes colorful Latin American tastes with a classy setting. Chef Fernando Estrella's menu includes a wide range of meals such as ceviches, tacos, and grilled meats. The chic décor and outdoor patio enhance the whole eating experience, making it ideal for a fun evening with friends or a romantic supper.

The fashionable cafés and restaurants on Grand Cayman are more than simply places to eat; they are experiences that capture the island's gastronomic diversity and commitment to quality. Whether you prefer the freshness of seafood at Calypso Grill, Michelin-starred excellence at Blue by Eric Ripert, or a caffeine fix at Cayman Coffee Club, each culinary venue adds a layer of depth to your Grand Cayman vacation. Prepare for a voyage that transcends the tongue as you discover these culinary treasures, immersing you in the flavors, inventiveness, and hospitality that define the culinary landscape of this Caribbean jewel.

Must Try Grand Cayman island Dishes

Grand Cayman, with its turquoise oceans and gorgeous beaches, is not just a visual feast but also a gastronomic paradise where flavors come to life. The island's unique culinary culture represents a blend of

Caribbean, European, and worldwide influences, providing tourists with a palate-pleasing trip. Here is a list of must-try Grand Cayman meals that capture the spirit of the island's culinary delights.

1. **A Caribbean Delicacy: Conch Fritters

Conch fritters are a Caribbean dish that entices seafood lovers to go on a gastronomic adventure. These fritters are a crunchy delicacy made with locally obtained conch, a species of sea mollusk. Before being deep-fried to golden perfection, the conch is carefully diced and combined with a variety of spices, herbs, and batter. Conch fritters, served with a zesty dipping sauce, highlight the island's devotion to fresh, ocean-to-table cuisine.

2. **A Savory Island Staple: Cayman-Style Beef

Cayman-Style Beef is a flavorful island favorite that combines Caribbean and foreign ingredients. The recipe comprises delicious beef marinated in a fragrant spice and herb combination then slow-cooked to exquisite perfection. Cayman-Style Beef, sometimes eaten with rice and beans, is a substantial and tasty meal that pleases both residents and visitors. Slow cooking allows the spices to penetrate the meat, resulting in a meal that embodies Caymanian culinary traditions.

3. **A Flavorful Caribbean Classic Jerk Chicken

No trip to the Caribbean is complete without sampling the legendary Jerk Chicken, and Grand Cayman does not disappoint. This tasty dish is made by marinating chicken in a spicy jerk seasoning blend, which includes Scotch bonnet peppers, allspice, thyme, and other fragrant spices. The chicken is then slow-cooked or grilled until soft and imbued with smokey, spicy, and fragrant characteristics. Jerk Chicken is a delectable Caribbean staple that shows the island's fondness for rich and powerful tastes when served with traditional sides like rice and beans or fried plantains.

4. A Culinary Heritage: Cayman Turtle Stew

Cayman Turtle Stew is a dish that embodies the island's culinary traditions. Turtles were numerous in the seas surrounding Grand Cayman in the past, and turtle stew became a popular delicacy. While sea turtle consumption is now restricted to conserve the species, some restaurants offer a contemporary variation on Cayman Turtle Stew with other ingredients. A thick broth laced with herbs and spices is generally utilized in the meal, producing a flavorful and soothing gastronomic experience.

5. Fish Tea: A Filling Seafood Soup

Fish Tea is a savory seafood stew that warms the spirit while also highlighting the island's relationship to the abundant Caribbean Sea. This classic Caymanian soup is made with a delectable combination of local fish, veggies, and spices that have been cooked to perfection. For a mild kick, the soup is frequently flavored with pepper and Scotch bonnet. Fish Tea, served hot with bread or fritters, is a hearty and filling dish that showcases the island's devotion to fresh and locally produced products.

6. **A Flavorful Seafood Delight: Cayman-Style Escovitch Fish**

Cayman-Style Escovitch Fish is a colorful and tasty seafood delicacy that exemplifies the island's penchant for robust and sour tastes. The meal is typically served with fried fish, such as snapper, and a colorful variety of pickled vegetables, including carrots, onions, and bell peppers. The escovitch sauce, created with vinegar and spices, gives the meal a zesty edge. Cayman-Style Escovitch Fish is a visual and gastronomic feast that embodies Caribbean cuisine with a Caymanian touch.

7. **Breadfruit: A Local Food with Versatile Applications

Breadfruit, while not a meal in and of itself, is a local staple with flexible possibilities that exemplifies the island's devotion to sustainable and locally derived foods. This starchy fruit, which has a texture comparable to potatoes, is commonly used in Caymanian recipes. Breadfruit can be fried, roasted, or boiled to make a tasty side dish or the primary ingredient in meals like breadfruit chips or breadfruit salad. Its flexibility and versatility in many culinary applications make it a must-try item that gives a distinct flavor to many regional meals.

8. **A Tropical Seafood Indulgence with Coconut Shrimp

Coconut Shrimp from Grand Cayman is a tropical seafood treat that mixes the sweetness of coconut with the succulence of shrimp. The shrimp are coated in a light batter, wrapped in shredded coconut, then deep-fried till crisp and golden brown. Coconut Shrimp, served with a dipping sauce, is a delicious combination of textures and flavors that exemplifies the island's devotion to create meals that highlight the wealth of the Caribbean.

9. **Mahi-Mahi: A Delicious Ocean Catch

The fresh and savory taste of Mahi-Mahi, a favorite ocean catch in the waters surrounding Grand Cayman, is appreciated. This white-fleshed fish is frequently grilled, charred, or pan-seared to perfection, enabling the inherent tastes of the fish to show through. Mahi-Mahi, served with a range of sauces ranging from mango salsa to citrus-infused glazes, captures the flavor of the Caribbean's abundant seafood options.

10. **Rundown: A Culinary Delight With Coconut**

Rundown is a coconut-infused gastronomic pleasure inspired by Grand Cayman's tropical tastes. This traditional meal is made with fish or shellfish that has been cooked in a creamy coconut milk broth and seasoned with a combination of indigenous herbs and spices. Slow simmering allows the components to mingle, resulting in a flavorful and fragrant stew. Rundown is a cozy and savory dish that pays respect to the island's culinary origins. It is often served with bread or dumplings.

The culinary landscape of Grand Cayman is a celebration of tastes inspired by the island's rich cultural past and the bounty of the Caribbean Sea. Each meal conveys a tale of the island's culinary traditions and devotion to fresh, locally produced ingredients, from the savory joys of Cayman-Style Beef to the vivid and spicy overtones of Jerk Chicken. Prepare to sample the various and scrumptious delicacies that make this Caribbean paradise a veritable refuge for food connoisseurs as you start on a gourmet excursion in Grand Cayman.

Shopping Centers and Street Markets

1. **Camana Bay**

Address: 10 Market St, Camana Bay, George Town, Cayman Islands.

Camana Bay, located in the heart of Grand Cayman, offers a vibrant mix of upscale shops, boutiques, restaurants, and entertainment options. With its picturesque waterfront setting, visitors can stroll along the promenade, browse unique stores offering everything from fashion and accessories to home décor, and enjoy dining with views of the bay. The Town Centre hosts regular events, including live music concerts, farmers' markets, and outdoor movie screenings, adding to the lively atmosphere. Camana Bay is not just a shopping destination; it's a cultural hub where locals and tourists alike gather to shop, dine, relax, and enjoy the best of Grand Cayman's lifestyle.

2. **The Strand Shopping Centre**

Address: West Bay Rd, Seven Mile Beach, Grand Cayman, Cayman Islands.

Situated along Seven Mile Beach, The Strand Shopping Centre offers a diverse array of shops, restaurants, and entertainment options. Visitors can explore a mix of local boutiques and international brands, dine at waterfront restaurants, and catch a movie at the cinema. The center's beachfront location provides stunning views and a relaxed atmosphere for shopping and leisure.

3. **Governor's Square**

Address: 23 Lime Tree Bay Ave, Seven Mile Beach, Grand Cayman, Cayman Islands.

Governor's Square is a popular shopping plaza in Seven Mile Beach, offering a wide range of shops, restaurants, and services. Visitors can shop for clothing, jewelry, and souvenirs, dine at various eateries, and enjoy entertainment options. The plaza's central location makes it convenient for visitors staying in the Seven Mile Beach area to access shopping and dining amenities.

4. **Bayshore Mall**

Address: Harbour Dr, George Town, Cayman Islands.

Bayshore Mall, located in George Town, is a bustling shopping destination offering a mix of local and international retailers, restaurants, and entertainment options. Visitors can explore a variety of shops selling fashion, electronics, and souvenirs, dine at waterfront restaurants, and enjoy live music performances. The mall's waterfront location provides scenic views of George Town Harbor, adding to the overall shopping experience.

5. **Foster's Food Fair - Strand**

Address: 3139 West Bay Rd, George Town, Grand Cayman, Cayman Islands.

Foster's Food Fair - Strand is a supermarket chain that also offers a selection of clothing, household items, and souvenirs alongside its grocery offerings. Visitors can shop for groceries and household essentials while also browsing a range of other products. The store's convenient location on West Bay Road makes it easily accessible for both residents and tourists staying in the area.

6. **Cayman Craft Market**

Address: 57 North Church St, George Town, Grand Cayman, Cayman Islands.

The Cayman Craft Market, located in George Town, showcases the work of local artisans and craftsmen, offering handmade goods including jewelry, artwork, and souvenirs. Visitors can explore stalls filled with unique and authentic Caymanian products, interact with local artisans, and purchase one-of-a-kind souvenirs to take home. The market's vibrant atmosphere and cultural significance make it a must-visit destination for those interested in experiencing the local arts and crafts scene.

7. **Queen's Court Plaza**

Address: West Bay Rd, Seven Mile Beach, Grand Cayman, Cayman Islands.

Queen's Court Plaza, situated in Seven Mile Beach, is a shopping complex featuring a variety of shops, restaurants, and services. Visitors can shop for clothing, accessories, and gifts, dine at restaurants offering diverse cuisines, and enjoy leisure activities. The plaza's convenient location along West Bay Road makes it easily accessible for visitors staying in the Seven Mile Beach area.

8. **Galleria Plaza**

Address: West Bay Rd, Seven Mile Beach, Grand Cayman, Cayman Islands.

Galleria Plaza, located in Seven Mile Beach, offers a mix of shops, restaurants, and services catering to both locals and tourists. Visitors can shop for clothing, accessories, and souvenirs, dine at various eateries, and access essential services such as pharmacies and banks. The plaza's central location along West Bay Road makes it a convenient shopping destination for visitors exploring the Seven Mile Beach area.

9. **Heritage Square**

Address: Cardinal Ave, George Town, Grand Cayman, Cayman Islands.

Heritage Square, situated in George Town, is a shopping complex featuring a variety of shops, restaurants, and entertainment options. Visitors can explore shops selling clothing, jewelry, and gifts, dine at restaurants offering local and international cuisines, and enjoy live music performances. The square's central location in George Town makes it easily accessible for visitors exploring the capital city's attractions and landmarks.

10. **Marquee Plaza**

Address: Lawrence Blvd, George Town, Grand Cayman, Cayman Islands.

Marquee Plaza, located in George Town, is a shopping and entertainment complex offering a mix of shops, restaurants, and leisure activities. Visitors can shop for clothing, electronics, and souvenirs, dine at restaurants offering diverse cuisines, and enjoy entertainment options such as cinemas and arcades. The plaza's central location in George Town makes it a convenient destination for visitors exploring the capital city's attractions and landmarks.

Tips for Dining and Shopping In Grand Cayman

When dining and shopping in Grand Cayman, travelers can immerse themselves in the vibrant local culture while savoring delicious cuisine and discovering unique treasures. Here are some tips to enhance your dining and shopping experience on the island:

Dining Tips:
1. **Sample Local Cuisine**: Grand Cayman offers a diverse culinary scene influenced by Caribbean, British, and international flavors. Don't miss the opportunity

to sample local specialties such as conch fritters, Cayman-style fish, and jerk chicken.

2. **Explore Food Markets**: Visit local food markets like Camana Bay Farmers & Artisans Market or Cayman Islands Farmers Market to discover fresh produce, seafood, spices, and handmade crafts. These markets offer a glimpse into local life and provide opportunities to taste authentic flavors.

3. **Try Seafood**: With its abundant marine life, Grand Cayman is renowned for its fresh seafood. Head to waterfront restaurants or local seafood shacks to enjoy dishes like grilled mahi-mahi, lobster tail, and Caribbean fish stew.

4. **Indulge in Rum Tasting**: Grand Cayman is famous for its rum production. Visit a distillery or rum bar to sample a variety of locally distilled rums and learn about the island's rich rum-making heritage.

5. **Make Reservations**: Popular restaurants in Grand Cayman can get busy, especially during peak tourist seasons. Make reservations in advance to secure your table and avoid disappointment.

Shopping Tips:

1. **Visit Local Markets**: Explore local markets such as Camana Bay Market Street or Cayman Craft

Market to find handmade crafts, artwork, jewelry, and souvenirs crafted by local artisans. These markets offer unique gifts and keepsakes to commemorate your trip.

2. **Explore Duty-Free Shopping:** Take advantage of duty-free shopping opportunities in George Town and Seven Mile Beach. Look for luxury goods, jewelry, watches, and electronics at discounted prices.

3. **Support Local Businesses:** Seek out locally owned shops and boutiques to support the island's economy and discover authentic Caymanian products. Look for stores selling handmade crafts, clothing, and accessories designed by local artisans.

4. **Bargain at Street Markets:** When shopping at street markets or independent vendors, don't be afraid to haggle for the best price. Negotiating is common practice in many markets and can result in significant savings.

5. **Check for VAT Refunds:** Visitors to Grand Cayman may be eligible for a refund of Value Added Tax (VAT) on certain purchases. Look for participating retailers and inquire about VAT refund procedures to maximize savings on your shopping purchases.

By following these tips, travelers can enjoy memorable dining experiences and discover unique treasures while shopping in Grand Cayman, creating lasting memories of their visit to the island.

Chapter Eight: Practical Advice For Visitors

Currency and Banking information

As you plan your trip to Grand Cayman, educate yourself with the island's currency and financial environment to guarantee a smooth and worry-free journey. The Cayman Islands Dollar (KYD) is the official currency of Grand Cayman, which is a British Overseas Territory. Understanding the currency exchange, banking facilities, and financial intricacies can make your stay on this Caribbean jewel more informed and pleasurable.

Currency: KYD (Cayman Islands Dollar)

The Cayman Islands Dollar (KYD) is the island's official currency. While the US dollar (USD) is commonly recognized across the island, it is crucial to remember that most local transactions are handled in Cayman Islands dollars. The KYD is locked to the USD, keeping the exchange rate stable and simple to compute. Both currencies are in use, and establishments frequently show pricing in both USD and KYD.

Exchange Rates: Where and How to Convert Money

On Grand Cayman, currency exchange is easily accessible, and travelers have various alternatives for converting their money.

1. **Banks:** Currency exchange services are provided by local banks such as Cayman National Bank, Butterfield Bank, and RBC Royal Bank. Weekday banking hours are normally from 9:00 a.m. to 4:00 p.m., with certain banks offering limited Saturday hours.

2. **Currency Exchange Offices:** Currency exchange offices are located in important tourist spots such as George Town and Seven Mile Beach. To accommodate travelers, these establishments frequently provide inexpensive prices and longer hours.

3. **ATMs:** ATMs are extensively available around the island, letting tourists withdraw local cash directly from their bank accounts. ATMs accept Cayman Islands Dollars, and most machines also accept USD withdrawals.

4. **Hotels & Resorts:** Certain hotels and resorts provide currency exchange services to its visitors. It is,

134

nevertheless, prudent to investigate the rates and expenses associated with these services.

When exchanging money, keep possible costs and exchange rates in mind, especially at airport kiosks or currency exchange offices. It is recommended that you check rates at several locations to ensure you receive the most value for your money.

Banking Services: Obtaining Financial Services

Grand Cayman has a well-established banking infrastructure that offers a variety of financial services and amenities to visitors.

1. **Banks:** On the island, major banks such as Cayman National Bank, Butterfield Bank, and RBC Royal Bank provide a variety of services such as currency exchange, ATM access, and individual financial help.

2. **ATMs:** ATMs may be found across Grand Cayman, allowing tourists to withdraw cash, check account balances, and conduct other financial operations. Check that your bank card is compatible with overseas ATMs and notify your bank of your trip intentions to minimize service delays.

3. **Credit Cards:** Most places on the island accept credit cards like Visa, MasterCard, and American Express. However, carrying cash is recommended, especially for smaller sellers or institutions in more rural places.

4. **Currency Withdrawal limitations:** Your bank may impose withdrawal limitations on your account. If you anticipate requiring a large sum of money, you should check with your bank ahead of time.

Banking Suggestions for Visitors:

1. **Inform Your Bank:** Before traveling to Grand Cayman, notify your bank of your trip dates and location to avoid any credit or debit card complications.

2. **Currency Preferences:** While both Cayman Islands Dollars and US Dollars are accepted, carrying a mix of both currencies is recommended for more flexibility.

3. **Check currency Rates:** Stay updated on currency rates to make better judgments when exchanging money.

4. **Emergency Contacts:** Keep a list of the emergency contact numbers for your bank in case your cards are lost or stolen.

5. **safe ATMs: When using ATMs, use machines that are well-lit and safe. Keep an eye on your surroundings and protect your PIN when entering it.

Understanding the currency and financial dynamics of Grand Cayman will make your vacation more pleasurable. Whether you're browsing local markets, dining in restaurants, or participating in aquatic sports, knowing about currency exchange and banking facilities will enhance your whole experience on this enthralling Caribbean island.

Safety precautions

When traveling to the lovely Grand Cayman Island, it is critical to prioritize safety in order to fully appreciate the natural beauty and rich culture that this Caribbean treasure has to offer. While Grand Cayman is recognized for its welcoming attitude and low crime rates, exercising care and awareness is vital for a worry-free and pleasurable vacation. Here is a list of safety measures that travelers should take while visiting this tropical paradise.

1. Water Safety: Responsibly Enjoying the Caribbean Waters

The turquoise seas of Grand Cayman are a key appeal for vacationers looking for sun, beach, and sea. While beaches and seas are typically safe, water safety should be practiced:

- **Beach Flags:** Keep an eye out for beach flags that indicate sea conditions. A red flag may indicate dangerous currents, therefore swim with caution or avoid such situations.
- **Snorkeling and Diving:** Before participating in aquatic sports, make sure you're in excellent health and follow the safety rules supplied by tour operators. Check your equipment before using it, and stay mindful of your surroundings.
- **Weather Awareness:** Pay close attention to weather forecasts, particularly during hurricane season (June to November). Keep up to date on any advisories and adhere to local regulations.

2. Sun Protection: Protecting Yourself from Tropical Rays

Because Grand Cayman has so much sunshine, sun protection is a primary priority:

- **Sunscreen:** Use a high SPF sunscreen on a frequent basis, especially if you plan to spend long amounts of time in the sun. Remember to apply again after swimming.
- **Hydration:** Drink plenty of water to stay hydrated, especially in hot weather. Avoid drinking too much alcohol, which can contribute to dehydration.
- **Protective gear:** To protect yourself from the sun, consider wearing protective gear such as a wide-brimmed hat and lightweight, long-sleeved clothes.

3. Wildlife Awareness: Protecting the Flora and Fauna of the Island

The marine and terrestrial fauna of Grand Cayman is varied. While interactions with animals can be thrilling, they must be approached with caution:
- **Coral Reefs:** When snorkeling or diving, avoid touching or standing on coral reefs. Coral is not only delicate, but some species can cause skin discomfort.
- **Stingrays:** Follow the recommendations offered by tour operators for safe interaction with these friendly creatures if visiting the famed Stingray City. Avoid unexpected movements and be aware of your surroundings.

- **fauna on Land:** Be mindful of the island's fauna, which includes iguanas and birds. Maintain a safe distance from them and refrain from feeding them, since this might alter their natural behavior.

4. Personal Belongings: Preventing Theft and Loss

While Grand Cayman is regarded safe, it is always prudent to take the following steps to safeguard your belongings:

- **Valuables:** Keep superfluous valuables, such as expensive jewelry and significant sums of money, in a safe place. Passports and travel papers should be kept in hotel safes.

- **Beach Bags:** Keep a watch on your valuables, especially if the beach is crowded. Keep basics in a waterproof bag and avoid leaving valuables unattended.

5. Local Laws and Customs: Following Grand Cayman's Rules

It is essential to become acquainted with local laws and customs in order to have a pleasant and polite visit:

- **Traffic Regulations:** Obey traffic regulations, such as driving on the left side of the road. Cross streets with caution and be mindful of local driving habits.

- **Drug Policies:** Grand Cayman has strong drug policies. Even little quantities of prohibited drugs might result in harsh consequences.

6. Precautions for Health: Prioritizing Your Well-Being During Your Stay

Maintaining good health is essential for a pleasurable travel experience:

- **Medical Services:** Learn where the island's medical facilities are located. Carry prescription drugs as well as a basic first-aid kit.

- **Mosquito Protection:** Take mosquito precautions, especially at dawn and dusk. In places with dense vegetation, use insect repellent and wear long sleeves and pants.

7. Emergency Contacts: Being Ready for Anything

Keep emergency contact information handy:

- **Emergency Numbers:** Be aware of the local emergency numbers, which include police, fire, and medical services (911).

- **Embassy Information:** If you require assistance, be aware of your country's embassy or consulate information.

By including these safety precautions in your vacation planning, you'll be well-equipped to thoroughly appreciate Grand Cayman Island's delights. Prioritizing safety will enhance your experience and ensure a great stay in this Caribbean paradise, whether you're lazing on its gorgeous beaches, exploring vivid coral reefs, or immersing yourself in local culture.

Contact and Emergency Information

Having access to important contact and emergency information is critical for a safe and pleasurable vacation to Grand Cayman Island. While the island is famed for its hospitality and safety, it's always a good idea to be prepared for any unexpected events. Here's a full list of contact and emergency numbers for guests to have handy throughout their stay:

1. **Emergency Medical Services:
- **Police:** Dial **911** in an emergency or if you require police help. The Royal Cayman Islands Police Service (RCIPS) is in charge of enforcing the law on the island.

- **Fire and Rescue:** Dial **911** for fire emergencies or rescue assistance.
- **Medical Emergencies:** Dial **911** if you require immediate medical help. Your location will be visited by emergency medical personnel.

2. **Hospitals and Medical Services:
- **George Town Hospital:** The Health Services Authority (HSA) in George Town is Grand Cayman's principal hospital. It offers a variety of medical services, including emergency treatment.
- **Address:** 95 Hospital Road, George Town, Cayman Islands
- Phone: +1 (345) 949-8600
- **Cayman Islands Hospital:** This hospital provides comprehensive healthcare services as well as emergency services.

3. **Pharmacies:
- **Professional Pharmacy:** This pharmacy, located in George Town, offers a variety of prescription and over-the-counter drugs.
- **Address:** 34 Hospital Road, George Town, Cayman Islands
- Phone: +1 (345) 949-7388

- **Foster's Pharmacy:** Foster's Pharmacy is a handy alternative for pharmaceutical requirements, with various sites over the island.

4. **Embassy and Consulate Contacts:
- **US Embassies and Consulates:**
- 150 Smith Road, George Town, Cayman Islands
- **Telephone: +1 (345) 945-8173
- **High Commission of the United Kingdom:**
- **Address:** 103 South Church Street, George Town, Grand Cayman Business Centre, 2nd Floor
- **Telephone:** +1 (345) 244-2433

5. CITA (Cayman Islands Tourism Association):
- **CITA Visitor Information Centre:** This location provides general tourism information, guidance, and suggestions.
- 1320 West Bay Road, George Town, Cayman Islands
- Phone: +1 (345) 949-8522

6. **Services of Transportation:
- **Taxis:** Taxis are plentiful on the island. Look for certified cabs that have the proper taxi license displayed.

- **vehicle Rentals:** On Grand Cayman, several vehicle rental firms operate, providing handy alternatives for exploring the island at your own leisure.
- **Public Transportation:** The Cayman Islands Public Bus Service is an inexpensive way to get about the island.

8. **Local Weather Forecast:
- **National meteorological Service:** Stay up to date on meteorological conditions, particularly during hurricane season (June to November).
- **Telephone: +1 (345) 946-4999

9. **Lost or Stolen Property:
- **Royal Cayman Islands Police Service (RCIPS):** Contact the police if you find any lost or stolen things.
- Phone: +1 (345) 949-4222

10. **Airport Specifics:
- **Owen Roberts International Airport (GCM):** For airport information and services.
- Phone: +1 (345) 949-5252

11. **Tourist Information Line:
- **Cayman Islands Tourism Department:** For general visitor information and support.
- Phone: +1 (345) 949-0623

Having this contact and emergency information on hand will help to ensure a safe and well-prepared visit to Grand Cayman Island. While the island is famed for its quiet and warmth, being informed of local services and emergency protocols allows you to completely enjoy your time in this Caribbean paradise with peace of mind.

Souvenirs to Bring Home

As you bask in Grand Cayman Island's sun-drenched splendor, you'll discover that the charm of this Caribbean paradise extends far beyond its beautiful beaches and crystal-clear waters. The colorful culture and rich past of the island are beautifully reflected in a plethora of souvenirs that make ideal recollections of your tropical holiday. Whether you're a collector, a fashionista, or a fan of local workmanship, Grand Cayman has a wide range of gifts that encapsulate the essence of this fascinating island.

1. Caymanite Jewelry:

Caymanite is a semi-precious stone that can only be found in the Cayman Islands. Caymanite, known for its beautiful patterns and warm colors, is frequently used to produce exquisite jewelry items. This local stone may be found in rings, earrings, pendants, and bracelets, making for a one-of-a-kind and significant keepsake.

2. **Rum Cake Tortuga:**

Indulge your taste senses and bring a bit of the Caribbean home with you with a **Tortuga Rum Cake**. These exquisite sweets are created with the best Caribbean rum, resulting in a moist and tasty cake that embodies the spirit of the islands. Tortuga Rum Cakes, available in original, chocolate, and coconut flavors, are a delightful memento of your tropical getaway.

3. **Sand Jewelry from Seven Mile Beach:**

Seven Mile Beach is well-known not just for its beautiful beachfront, but also for its distinctive sand. This sand is used by island artisans to produce gorgeous jewelry pieces like necklaces and bracelets. You can take a piece of Grand Cayman's renowned beach with you wherever you go with these wearable gems.

4. **Sculptures in Caymanite:

Caymanite is used to produce elaborate sculptures that exhibit the artistic ability of local craftsmen, in addition to jewelry. These sculptures, which range from marine life to abstract patterns, capture the natural splendor of the Cayman Islands. A Caymanite sculpture is a beautiful and timeless work of art that will add a touch of the Caribbean to your house.

5. **Local Paintings & Artwork:

Bring home a piece of local artwork to immerse yourself in Grand Cayman's dynamic arts scene. Many excellent painters live on the island, and their works frequently portray the spectacular scenery, marine life, and culture of the Cayman Islands. Local artwork, whether it's a vibrant painting or a one-of-a-kind sculpture, is a meaningful and visually appealing keepsake.

6. **Cayman Chili Sauce:

With a bottle of **Cayman Pepper Sauce**, you can spice up your culinary experiences at home. This spicy sauce, made with locally grown peppers, lends a tasty bite to foods and serves as a delectable reminder of the robust flavors of the Caribbean. Select from a variety of heat levels and appreciate the flavor of Grand Cayman in every drop.

7. **Caribbean-style Dress:

Pick up Caribbean-style apparel to add a bit of island flair to your outfit. From breezy sundresses to brilliant sarongs, the local stores provide a variety of apparel products that represent Grand Cayman's laid-back and colorful culture. Choose textiles that will keep you cool in the tropical heat while also giving a Caribbean flair to your look.

8. **Jewelry made of sea glass:

The beaches of Grand Cayman are studded with smooth, naturally tumbling shards of sea glass. Local artists turn these ocean treasures into one-of-a-kind jewelry pieces such as earrings, pendants, and bracelets. Each piece of **sea glass jewelry** carries marine energy and serves as a lovely and meaningful keepsake.

9. **Homemade Rum and Spirits:

Consider taking home a bottle of **local rum or spirits** for those who enjoy a nice libation. The Cayman Islands have their own distilleries, which produce rum with unique characteristics. Explore the diversity of locally created spirits, such as flavored rums and unusual mixes, to enjoy the Caribbean long after your visit has ended.

10. **Flags and Emblems of the Cayman Islands:

Bring home a memento with the Cayman Islands' national flag or emblem to show off your affection for the islands. These insignia, whether on a keychain, a magnet, or a decorative object, serve as a patriotic memento of your stay on this Caribbean island.

Consider the unique tales and cultural importance of each item while purchasing Grand Cayman souvenirs. Whether it's Caymanite, the tastes of local rum, or the artistic interpretations of the island's brilliant craftsmen, these mementos become more than simply tokens; they become treasured keepsakes of the moments made in this tropical paradise.

Conclusion

As we close the curtain on our tour of Grand Cayman, it's clear that this Caribbean gem offers much more than sun-kissed beaches and blue oceans. We've gone into the heart of Grand Cayman's complex tapestry via the pages of this travel book, revealing a paradise that flawlessly mixes natural beauty, cultural vibrancy, and friendly hospitality. The charm of Grand Cayman grips you from the moment you foot onto the island, weaving an everlasting tapestry of memories that remain long after the tan lines have faded.

Grand Cayman is more than a holiday destination; it's a haven of peace, a place where time pauses and nature takes center stage. The beautiful landscapes of the island, whether the famed Seven Mile Beach, the brilliant coral reefs, or the lush interiors, serve as a canvas painted with hues of peace and adventure. Each part of this guide has attempted to peel back the layers of Grand Cayman's attraction, providing tips on how to plan your trip, navigate the island's culture and customs, and indulge in its gastronomic wonders.

Grand Cayman shows itself as a harmonic combination of tradition and development, from the echoes of the island's history to the pulse of its modern existence. Visitors are drawn not just by the appeal of its natural beauty, but also by the kindness of its inhabitants, who kindly share their island paradise's secrets. Whether immersed in the vibrant traditions of local festivals, savoring the flavors of Caribbean cuisine, or exploring the depths of the crystal-clear waters, Grand Cayman is a destination that invites you to be present, savor each moment, and forge connections that transcend time.

Consider the things you bring with you when you leave Grand Cayman—they are more than simply mementos; they are reminders of a voyage that extends beyond the physical. The Caymanite jewelry, Tortuga Rum Cake, sea glass jewelry, and bright artworks are more than just decorative things; they are windows into memories of leisurely days on sandy beaches, laughing of newfound friends, and whispers of a soft sea breeze. Souvenirs from Grand Cayman become storytellers, telling the tales of your Caribbean adventure.

This book was designed to serve as your compass, leading you through the complexities of planning, the nuances of local traditions, and the kaleidoscope of activities that Grand Cayman has to offer. Grand Cayman has been your gracious host, giving a symphony of experiences that resonate individually with each tourist, whether you sought adventure in the depths of the ocean, immersed yourself in the island's cultural tapestry, or just savored in the bliss of leisure.

Grand Cayman is more than a vacation destination; it is a celebration of nature's beauties and human relationships. It's a blank canvas begging to be painted with your distinct exploration and discovery strokes. May your recollections of Grand Cayman serve as a reminder that, in this enthralling corner of the Caribbean, time stops still for moments that truly count. May the spirit of Grand Cayman stay in your heart until the next chapter of your journey begins, enticing you to return to its shores and create fresh tales of sunsets, sea turtles, and the eternal charm of paradise.

Related Books

Expand your exploration beyond Loreto and delve into the enchanting wonders of Cayman Brac and Little Cayman islands with our companion guide. Discover iconic landmarks, hidden gems, and insider tips to make the most of your journey throughout Cayman. Simply scan the QR code below to access the Cayman Brac and Little Cayman islands Travel Guide and embark on a seamless adventure through those must visit destinations in Cayman Island.

Cayman Brac Island Travel Guide

Little Cayman Travel Guide

Travel Journal

Grand Cayman Travel Journal

Date: _____ Transport: _____

Weather

Amazing things you saw in Grand Cayman island

Places:

Notes

I am Grateful For The Opportunity To See the world

Grand Cayman Travel Journal

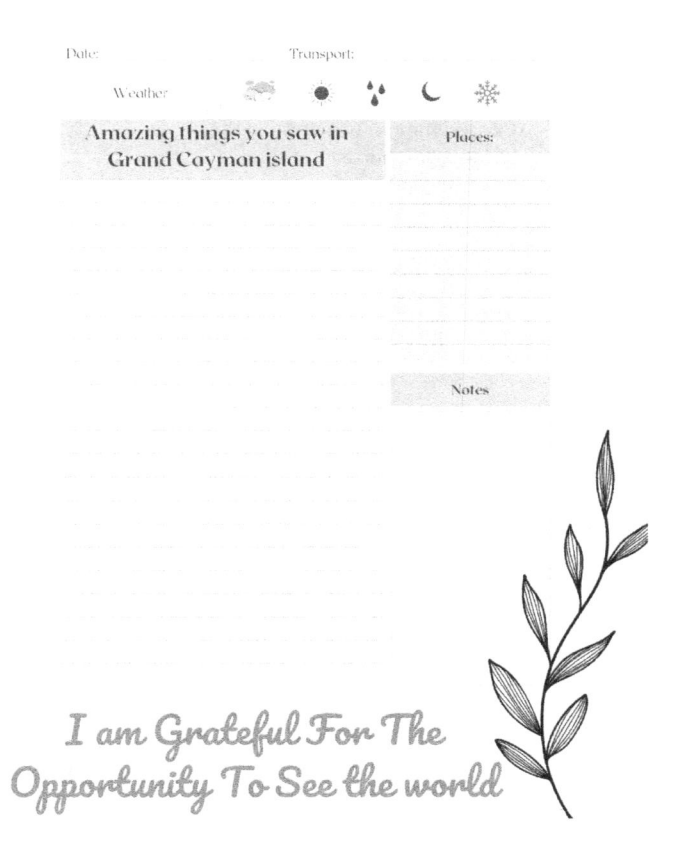

Date: Transport:

Weather:

Amazing things you saw in Grand Cayman island	Places:
	Notes

I am Grateful For The Opportunity To See the world

Grand Cayman Travel Journal

Date: _____ Transport: _____

Weather: 🌥 ☀ 💧 🌙 ❄

Amazing things you saw in Grand Cayman island	Places:
	Notes

I am Grateful For The Opportunity To See the world

Grand Cayman Travel Journal

Date: Transport:

Weather:

Amazing things you saw in Grand Cayman island	Places:

Notes

I am Grateful For The Opportunity To See the world

Grand Cayman Travel Journal

Date: _____   Transport: _____

Weather

Amazing things you saw in Grand Cayman island

Places:

Notes

I am Grateful For The Opportunity To See the world

Grand Cayman Travel Journal

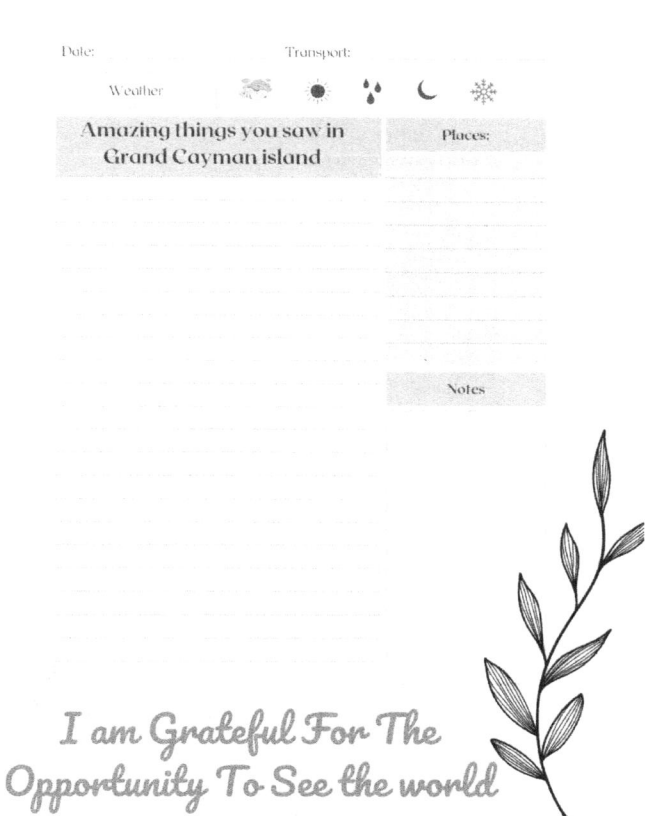

Date: Transport:

Weather:

Amazing things you saw in Grand Cayman island	Places:

Notes

I am Grateful For The Opportunity To See the world

Grand Cayman Travel Journal

Date: Transport:

Weather

Amazing things you saw in Grand Cayman island

Places:

Notes

I am Grateful For The Opportunity To See the world

Grand Cayman Travel Journal

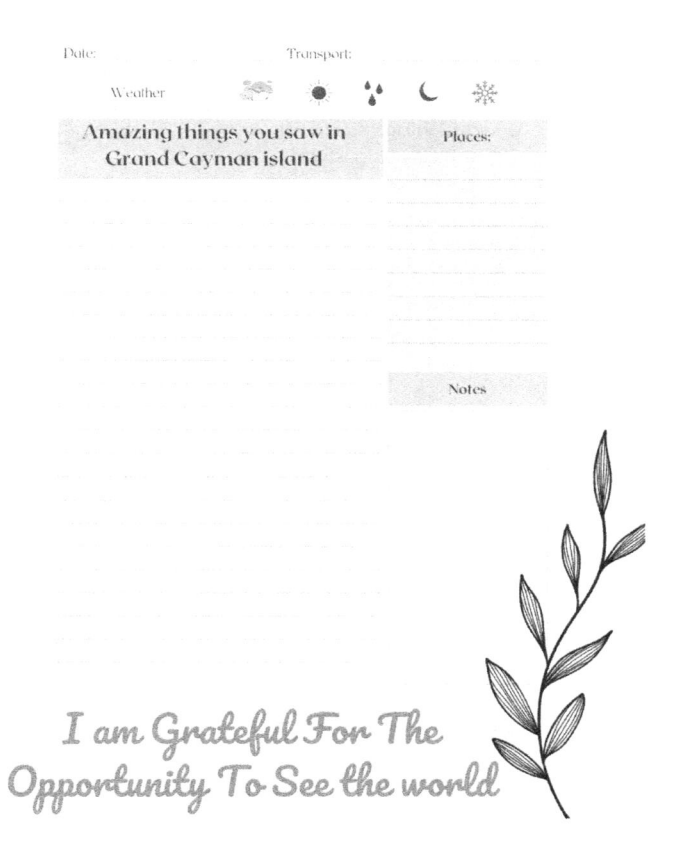

Date: Transport:

Weather

Amazing things you saw in Grand Cayman island

Places:

Notes

I am Grateful For The Opportunity To See the world

Grand Cayman Travel Journal

Date: Transport:

Weather

Amazing things you saw in Grand Cayman island	Places:

Notes

I am Grateful For The Opportunity To See the world

Grand Cayman Travel Journal

Date: Transport:

Weather

Amazing things you saw in Grand Cayman island

Places:

Notes

I am Grateful For The Opportunity To See the world

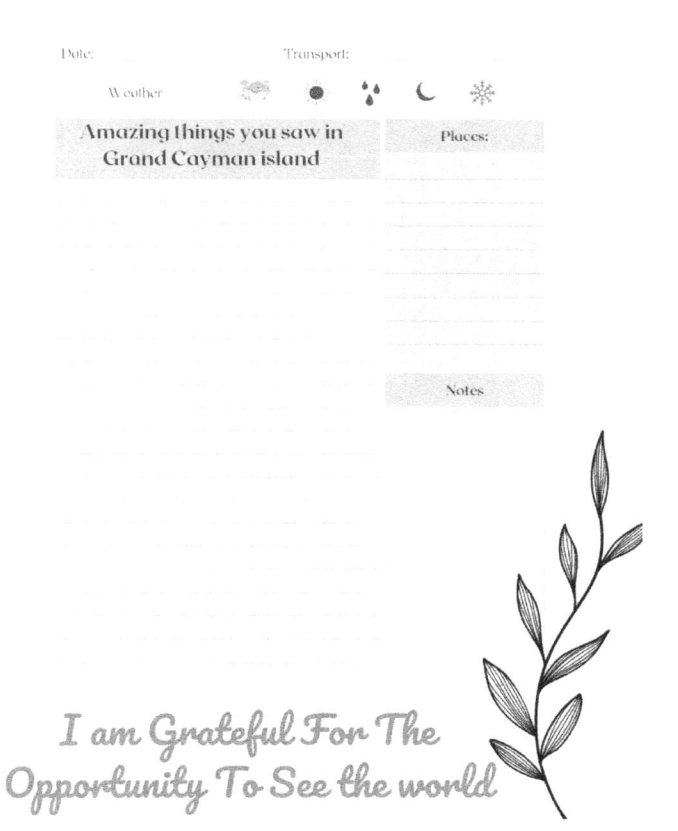

Made in the USA
Monee, IL
22 April 2025